Pra

My Side of the Bed

"After thirty-five years of marriage, Margherita Gale Harris learned about the secret her husband had been keeping for all those years. Part of her recovery from the betrayal, anguish, uncertainty, grief, and loss was to create this beautifully written and heart-wrenching memoir. This book describes in detail how she was impacted and how she eventually was able to build a new life. It also describes her years-long struggle to get recognition from the Episcopal Church of her suffering and her need to get her marriage annulled."

—Jennifer Schneider MD, PhD,
Author of *Back from Betrayal*

"*My Side of the Bed* is a survivor's tale—full of anguish, anger, passion, and finally healing. From moving on from a loveless marriage to standing up to the Episcopal Church, Harris shows her strong spirit in a way that's inspiring and timely."

—Elizabeth Fishel
Coauthor of *Getting to 30*

"*My Side of the Bed* is [Gale's] transformational story of . . . emotional abandonment in childhood, sexual betrayal throughout her marriage, and serious errors of omission within the power structure of her mainstream Christian denomination."

—Pamela H. Netzow
Friend of many years
and spiritual confidant

My Side of the Bed

A Memoir of Deceit, Denial
and Discovery

Margherita Gale Harris

My Side of the Bed: A Memoir of Deceit, Denial and Discovery

Published by Wheatmark®
2030 East Speedway Boulevard, Suite 106
Tucson, Arizona 85719
www.wheatmark.com

Cover Art: Suz Galloway
birchbriarstudios.com

ISBN: 978-1-62787-522-6 (paperback)
ISBN: 978-1-62787-592-9 (hardcover)
ISBN: 978-1-62787-523-3 (ebook)
LCCN: 2017948468

rev201801
rev201802

Author's Note

Except in the case of well-known figures introduced by first and last names, I have changed names and other identifying details to respect personal privacy. I have also changed several place names.

This is my journey in its fullest truth as I remember it. Some of the dialogue and memories were based on written materials, some were based on my journals, and still others on conversations I had with other individuals.

My memoir is perhaps best understood when read in the context of the social stigmas prevalent during the last half of the twentieth century. If encountered today, many of the unspoken taboos that are woven into the fabric of my story would be discussed openly. Information technology has transformed our lives.

I have written my story because I hope it will be an instrument for positive change in the lives of the people who read it. If you find that it is, please pay it forward.

This book is dedicated to my brave and forgiving children and to my sailor husband. Thank you for your love, understanding, and for your patience when I had lost mine.

Rumi said that the light enters you at the bandaged place.

—Andrew Solomon

The plumber was digging around in the pipes

& he saw something shine in the muck & it

turned out to be the soul of the last

tenant.

He gave it to me & I said I wonder how we

can return it & he shrugged & said he found

stuff like that all the time. You'd be amazed

at what people lose, he said.

—Brian Andreas, *Mostly True: Collected Stories and Drawings*, IBSN 0-96426660-0-8

Contents

Foreword

Thomas Doyle, JCD, CADC

This is the story of the life and death of a relationship known in societal officialdom as "marriage." But, compared to the standard Christian and traditional secular models, a relationship it was, a marriage it was not.

As the years came and went the author painfully faced the realization that the person she had pledged her vows to was, in reality, someone else. The focal point of the story is the male partner's sexual identity. Revealing to a spouse that one was actually homosexual was a rare and daunting task during a period when some areas of society, including religious bodies, gave lip service to the acceptance of a gay orientation. Beneath the façade there was a deeply rooted conviction that having an unconventional (for the time) sexual orientation was not only wrong, but evil.

The male partner was an Episcopal priest and the author a devout Episcopalian woman committed to her church's culture and tradition. She was in for a rude and shocking awakening when she approached the leadership of her church, expecting help and getting instead a very cold shoulder. She revealed that her husband not only had sexual relationships with men, but also with underage boys—a crime in every state of the union. In one of her conversations with a pastoral and compassionate woman priest, the author is told the church "doesn't do well" in dealing with divorce. This of course is a stunner because any church man or woman worth anything should know how to properly respond to the one life event that brings more pain to individuals and families than any other.

My Side of the Bed points out a lot of truths, but the one I zeroed in on was the hypocrisy and useless-ness of the church leaders who, instead of trying to bring healing—as is their mission—brought instead a deepening of the pain that was already in the extreme. Their failure to respond to the author and their failure to acknowledge the criminal nature of some of the male partner's actions is an indictment of the systemic ineptitude of the hierarchical leadership of her denom-ination—a condition which, as we are now painfully aware, is shared by many other denominations.

Preface

Every generation wrestles with expectations and realities. Mine was no exception. Many of the moral and social attitudes that existed when I was younger have receded into the background. But not so long ago, some of those norms were taboos that could ruin careers and destroy families.

This story is my account of how the underpinnings and upheavals of society—with its secrets and its threats—unhinged my life and challenged me to construct another. It begins before the 1941 bombing of Pearl Harbor and continues into the twenty-first century.

World War II ended the Great Depression and left in its wake many changes and consequences. Over eighty-five million lives were lost. Globally, new borders and new countries were formed. In the United States, families moved nearer to the cities. Suburbs and malls appeared overnight. The culture we knew, replete with constraints, was about to be revolutionized. Social and psychological boundaries transformed. Humankind had lost its innocence.

During this time, cultural patterns were shifting: from women's place being in the home to the feminist movement; from the stigma of being an unwed mother to single parenting by choice; from deeply hidden sexual preferences to gay-rights parades. People were beginning to live openly diverse lives and wanted to be respected. As Dylan's song says, "The Times They Are a-Changin'."

My own parents, who had lived and married in Chicago, moved to Wisconsin. Dad told Mom that the people in Madison mowed their own lawns. He thought it was a place where children could grow up believing life was manageable.

Both my younger brother and I were baptized in the Episcopal Church, but starting in first grade my mother, a devout Christian Scientist, enrolled me in the Christian Science Sunday school. It was there I was told that God is love and that all mankind was made in His image and likeness. I was also told that being ill was the result of erroneous thinking. So when my throat felt tight and I couldn't catch my breath, when I started to shake and was afraid I was going to die, I believed there must be an error in my reasoning. I must be the error, and there must be something very wrong with me.

I didn't know it then, but that message hid in the core of my anxiety and panic attacks.

It wasn't until years later, when I got a rude wake-up call—a shattered marriage and a broken family—that

I had to come to terms with how anxiety was running my life.

I still tremble from time to time. Sometimes, I ask for help. After all, what is anxiety but the basic need to feel accepted and valued by another human being?

Acknowledgement

There are many who helped me to heal and to write this memoir. I think you know who you are, and to respect your privacy, I have not named you herein. But I want to remind you that without your continued concern, support and good humor, I don't know if I would have survived to write this story. I owe all of you a debt of gratitude.

I will, however, take this opportunity to thank a number of groups that helped me to heal: Spiritual Women, Al-Anon, Quest, the Tuesday Night Writer's Group, the Grief Recovery Program, Stephen's Ministry, the UCLA Writer's Seminar, my local art center, and members of my yoga classes. I also thank those attorneys, physicians, and other professionals who took me seriously and provided unwavering support.

And to my friends: Thank You! Many of you I've known since childhood, others from summer camp experiences, and still others from secondary school, college, and nursing school days. Some of you I met along the road of sadness, others along the path out of the darkness.

Thank you all for your kindness and willingness to listen. As Maya Angelou said, "there is no greater agony than bearing an untold story inside of you."

I am a part of all that I have met.

—Alfred Lord Tennyson

Prologue

I've been a terrible mother, she said as she leaned slightly forward in Dad's old upholstered armchair. Will you ever forgive me?

I took a quick breath and swallowed hard as I tried to hold back my tears. Mom reached for the Kleenex box on the mahogany piecrust table next to her and handed me a tissue as she blew her nose.

I felt the jailer had set me free. What's to forgive, Mom? It's all over now. It's all okay. Don't worry.

It wasn't until then that I realized how tiny and frail she was. Her high cheekbones were flushed, and her dark, curly hair was streaked with silver. I watched as she put on her rimless glasses. The spare oxygen tank was nestled next to her chair.

Was it...was I really that bad? she said.

I could hardly hear her whisper and leaned forward to catch her words. For a split second, old wounds churned within me as I wondered what had made her change. Then, realizing I'd never know for certain, I said, No, Mom, not really. Look at all the folks we've known: some were alcoholics, some committed suicide, and some had several dads. I'm not walking the streets, so no, it wasn't that bad.

Do you want to talk about it now, she said, running her hands over her blue silk robe.

Not really. I don't know what I'd say. We've been at it so long, and suddenly I don't feel so angry anymore. I relaxed into the sofa. It was the first time in my entire life I could remember feeling comfortable with her.

The living-room curtains were drawn back, and the cool warmth of the Indian summer sun spread across the thick beige carpet. Outside the window, the old horse-chestnut tree was almost bare. It was 1987. Dad had died seven years earlier. The house still felt empty without him.

If there's anything I can tell you that would help, she began to explain. I've buried a lot way down deep. Slipping her arm over the edge of the chair, she twisted her hand back and forth as if working a stake into the ground. Then, looking up at me, she sighed. I leave in a few weeks for California, you know. When I come back, after winter, if you think it would help, we can talk longer. I'll do anything that will make it easier for you or the children.

The late-afternoon sun touched her face. She was nearing eighty and still a stunning woman. Maybe we can learn to be playful with one another, she said, giving me a small smile.

I'd like that, Mom.

We continued talking for another hour, and I almost

forgot that we'd never been friends. She wanted to hear about my kids and about me, and at last I was able to share with her without fear of reprisal. I remembered then how animated she could be, gesturing with her hands. I bent over to give her a kiss good-bye and caught the scent of her favorite perfume, Guerlain's Tea Rose. Our eyes met for the first time as equals.

Years later, as I lived through the painful events to come, I more fully understood the gift she gave me that day. But then, deep within my heart, her longed-for words and her willingness to accept me as I was had already begun to heal me. The sense of having a mother after all, of being valued and cared for, made me feel more confident, and I would need that self-assurance, as I was about to meet challenges that would threaten my life.

Mother and Me

Psychological health comes from acceptance
starting in early infancy of all that you are,
good and bad, dirty and clean, naughty and
nice, smart and stupid. . . . It means recognizing that although you are not perfect, you
are still worthy of love.

—*E. Golomb, PhD*

Driving home along the river late that day in October of
1987, I kept hearing Mom's words. Forgive me, forgive
me. My memory was full of the distance between us
and of the run-ins we'd had as I grew up. I remembered
how as a child I often had a feeling of not being safe,
not being good enough.

I was born in Chicago on a wintry night before
Christmas. I was two and a half when Mom sent me—
with a nanny—to visit my father's parents. The Toots,
I called them, who lived just outside the Beltway in
Virginia. Decades slipped by before I came across the

letters that my Grandma Toot had written to Mom during my stay. One of the letters was addressed to her in care of a hospital in Chicago. Strange, I thought: my mother was a Christian Scientist and didn't believe in doctors. Surely I could have stayed with her parents in Chicago.

One overcast fall day, several months after having visited my grandparents, I was playing tea party with my dolls when I sensed someone looking at me. I turned around to see my mother and another woman standing in the doorway.

I want you to meet Edith, my mother said. She's coming to live with us, to take care of you. My mother turned away, leaving me alone with this new person. I gazed at her with interest and a degree of trepidation.

Edith was taller than my mom, and her hair was almost all white. When she smiled at me, I thought she was an angel. I took her by the hand and pulled her toward my little cherry chifforobe. Opening its door, I proudly pointed to a row of pale pastel dresses. These are my clothes, I said. Even as a toddler, I knew that my mother thought clothes were important.

In early December 1941, Edith celebrated my third birthday with me. I picked out a frilly pink dress to wear. A few days later, hearing my mother cry, I scampered into the living room and saw my parents holding each other. A newspaper stamped with huge black letters lay in confusion on the coffee table. Years later, I realized that was the day Pearl Harbor had been bombed.

During the war years, we moved to Vinita, Oklahoma, while Dad served as a lieutenant commander of an air-force training school for glider pilots. Vinita wasn't like the Chicago I knew, which covered miles of the Lake Michigan shoreline. It was a lot smaller.

Dad found us a house. It had a porch. I had always lived in a tower before—an apartment house where I could peer out the window at the cars going back and forth down below. At our new home, I could swing on a sofa that hung from two big rings in the porch ceiling. If I squinted hard enough, I saw a flat line in the distance where the scorched brown earth met the sky.

Sometimes, when it blew hard, the wind scooped up the dry dirt and whirled it across the street. Frightened, I'd run inside to find Edith. With the promise of a chocolate-chip cookie and a glass of milk, she'd put her arms around me and lead me to the kitchen.

Edith didn't have her own room in Vinita, so we both slept in mine. She told me stories at night when Dad was away at the airfield. We giggled a lot. I always felt safe and cared for when I was with her. No matter what she was doing—fixing her hair, washing our clothes, or baking bread—she was the one I felt happiest with.

I tried to remember if my mother ever played with me, but I drew a blank. I recalled Dad at my bedtime singing "Pistol Packin' Mama." Edith said to him, You'd better not let her mother hear you singing that to Gale. Dad was the one who sat at my bedside and told me stories. And although I had lots of books, I could not picture my mother reading to me. Most of all, I couldn't remember Mom ever hugging me.

My brother, Will, was born in the summer of 1944. By that time, we were settled in Madison, Wisconsin. Edith offered to help my mother take care of Will, but Edith told me later that my mom refused, saying she wasn't going to lose Will the way she had lost me.

Edith had to leave me when I was six to care for her elderly uncle, who was prospecting for gold in Arizona. I was heartbroken to see her walking away from the house, my dad beside her carrying her suitcase. I ran down the front walk to say good-bye, clutching my favorite doll dressed in the plaid jumper Edith made for her. I wrapped her in a blanket and shoved her into Edith's hands. You have to take her with you, I pleaded. She'll keep you company.

Edith settled into the car seat and cradled my doll on her lap. Don't forget to write me, she said, and she held up her hand to wave good-bye. My best doll was the closest thing to myself that I could give her. I would hold Edith in my heart forever.

It wasn't long after Edith left that Mom announced, without any warning, that I would be going to camp. Dad put my trunk in the back of the car. Mom sat next to Dad, holding Will in her arms. Dad drove for a long time. It was a Saturday afternoon, and the Metropolitan Opera was playing on the radio. Why couldn't Mom pay some attention to me instead of Willie or the music? I was the one who was going to be away. Maybe she just wanted to get rid of me.

I leaned forward, pulling on Dad's shoulder. Please. Stop the car. I don't want to go, I begged.

Dad drove to the side of the road, stopped the car,

and looked at Mom. She told him to drive on. He sat quietly, waiting for other instructions. Tears jumbled around in my throat, and I felt sick to my stomach. I wanted to snuggle up next to Edith, but she was gone. Mother turned around and gave me a scowl. You are going to camp. They are expecting you this afternoon. I sank back in my seat. I knew I couldn't win. I wanted to bite her head off. I hoped that maybe we'd be in a car wreck and wouldn't get there, but Dad was a good driver. When I was four, I opened the car door while he was driving around a corner, but he grabbed me and saved my life. I knew he loved me, because I would have hit the pavement and died right then if he hadn't caught me. I didn't know for sure if Mom loved me, but she clearly loved my little brother a lot. She was always fussing with him, holding him, and making funny baby sounds.

As the years unfolded, not only did I feel neglected, but I was also in a continuing struggle with my mother. She picked away at me like a bantam hen. The list was long: my hair, weight, clothes, and friends. There was nothing I could do to please her. Even when I brought home straight A's, she found some way to undermine my achievement. She seldom praised me or expressed interest in what I was learning.

When I was eleven, she decided she didn't like my posture at the dinner table, so she made me sit holding a broom handle across my back to keep my spine straight. My pubescent breasts poked at my blouse, and I wanted to shrink under the table in embarrassment. Dad tried to come to my rescue, promising me I could have the Lionel electric train I longed for if my posture remained good after a month's time. I got the train; my posture at the table was impeccable. Yet my mother persisted in badgering me.

As I continued driving home along the river, I thought about my mother's tears. They wouldn't change the fact that I had felt unwanted for so many years, but now I knew my mother had accepted me; now I knew she loved me after all and that whatever happened hadn't been all my fault.

In the summer of 1951, when I was twelve years old, Mom decided to send me to a different camp, a Christian Science camp. Right before camp began, my dad told me I would be going east to a boarding school that fall—the same school my mother had attended. I remember crawling into his lap as he sat in his big, stuffed chair in our living room, pleading with him to let me stay at home. You don't get along with your mother was his brief reply. Send *her* away then, I thought, but I was too scared to say aloud what I really felt.

Halfway through the summer program, I awoke in middle of the night. My face felt hot, my stomach hurt, and my heart pounded against my ribs. I couldn't catch my breath. I grabbed the book by my bed, Mary Baker Eddy's *Science and Health with Key to the Scriptures*, and searched for my flashlight. If I could read it, maybe I would be okay. My Sunday school teacher taught me that my scary feelings were an error in my thinking. God is love, she told me. Over and over I repeated the Lord's Prayer—Father, Mother, God all harmonious— until I fell asleep. The sound of the morning bell woke me up. My flashlight was next to my pillow, and my book lay open on the floor.

For many years following my first anxiety attack, I sidestepped, danced, and ducked to avoid my anxiety, but it pursued me like a hungry lion. I hid it under false confidence and schoolgirl pranks: putting glue on the toilet seats in the faculty lounge, filching ice cream from the kitchen, and sitting outside on the dorm roof late at night. Sometimes I willed away the panic, and at times I almost forgot it. I would go months without a hint of apprehension, and then, with hurricane fury, an anxiety attack would leave me feeling breathless, weak, and ashamed. I didn't tell anyone how I sometimes choked and couldn't swallow—that sometimes I was afraid I'd die.

There was another thing I never told anyone, except my roommate junior year. She told me to be very careful. I was deeply in love with a young man from home. I was just sixteen at the time. Grant was supposed to be in college, but he was having emotional problems and had to go to a hospital. In the 1950s, people didn't talk about mental health. Grant's older brother tried to explain Grant's difficulties to me. He said Grant experienced the world differently from the way a lot of people did. Piecing together what he did and didn't say, I determined right then to become a doctor and to rid the world of mental illness. It has always amazed me how audacious and naïve I was at the time. I hadn't yet experienced how brutal the world could be.

As graduation neared, I knew I would be leaving

the girls who had become my sisters and the school that had been my home for five years. I handed in my senior English research project, which I had written about the causes of mental illness. I had worked diligently on it most of the spring semester, reading material that I didn't understand, and then I crashed. I refused to get out of bed one morning and ended up being sent to the infirmary. The doctor couldn't find anything wrong with me. Of course, I didn't mention my anxiety, which by now had tightly wound itself around my neck. I didn't know what it was. Every so often I would yawn, trying to get air into my lungs. No one seemed to notice.

The school doctor must have spoken to my parents, telling them I needed to see a shrink, because Dad made an appointment for me to see the head of psychiatry at the university. The psychiatrist asked me a few questions, but mostly he and Dad consulted with one another. We left with a prescription for orange pills called Thorazine. Years later, when I was in nursing school, I learned that Thorazine was used for patients suffering from schizophrenia, not anxiety attacks.

I took a pill that night. The doctor hadn't warned me it would react with beer, which I had drunk earlier on a date. The room began to spin. I stumbled down the hallway, groping my way to my father's bedroom. He told me to go back to bed. In the morning, I threw the orange pills in the john and watched as their peach color spread across the top of the water.

I became a consummate actress, hiding from the humiliation and embarrassment that crouched behind every corner. I had a good teacher: Mom had hidden

from Will and me that our dad was bipolar. We were in our twenties before Mom told us of Dad's diagnosis. He probably had been going up or down for years. Surely we had noticed his behavior, or did we learn how *not* to see? My focus was on my own feelings of desertion when from time to time Mom sent me to Edith's sister's home. Now I realize, of course, that Mom was trying to protect me and must have been scared: her husband's behavior was erratic, she had no siblings to talk to, and her parents lived in Chicago. She wouldn't have wanted to tell anyone; she probably felt ashamed, and then there was her Christian Science, which must have made it harder for her.

In the fall of 1956, I started college in Massachusetts. It didn't take me long to realize that I had made the wrong choice. I had assumed the college had a premed track, so when my advisor suggested that I major in chemistry, I said no way. I had taken summer sessions at my own state university and knew it had a premed track, so I decided to transfer there. When I came home for Christmas vacation, I presented my plan to my father. My mother overheard me talking and pranced into the living room. No daughter of mine is going to that university, she declared. People there have straw in their hair.

Snob, I thought. You didn't even go to college, and now you think you can tell me where to go?

You can't live here if you go to the university, she said, shaking her finger at me. Dad said nothing. I ran upstairs, packed an overnight bag, and left to stay with a friend's family until I found a live-in job as a mother's

helper. I registered for premed classes and commuted by bus between my job and campus. Every month my mom's father would send me a ten-dollar bill. Don't tell your mother, he'd write.

It was almost dark now, but the freeway lights weren't on yet. I remembered the time when I was still in boarding school, when my grandfather took me to his room and pointed to the photo of my mother and me on his desk. What went wrong there, Little Feller, what went wrong? he said. I held back my tears and shook my head. I said I didn't know.

Organic chemistry did me in. I was one of three women in a class of five hundred students. I didn't do well. I got my first D ever and thought that it ended my chances for medical school. I felt demoralized and didn't know which way to run. I wasn't welcome at home, and trying to return would be admitting I had made a mistake. I hadn't heard from Grant in almost a year, and I didn't want to ask any adult what had happened to him for fear I would learn something terrible.

In September 1957, I took the easy way out and transferred to a college in Boston. I started dating a young man, Richard, whom I had met briefly a year earlier. By the time May arrived, we'd been dating for more than half a year. Like most of the other couples in his fraternity, we explored the nuances of lovemaking, and in my naïveté, as we tumbled onto his narrow army cot one soft spring night, I didn't realize until we uncoupled that he wasn't wearing a condom. I knew right then that I was pregnant.

Six weeks later, our family doctor confirmed my pregnancy, and when I told him I was headed to California, he referred me to an obstetrician in San Francisco. I called Rick to give him the news. I was furious with him. Let's get married, he suggested. He said the right thing, but I didn't want to get married then.

I'm too young; I want to finish college. You don't have even have a job, I said. I felt deceived by Rick and trapped by my situation, but I knew I had made a mistake, so that meant it was my responsibility to fix it.

My mother would damn me for certain. As far as I was concerned, I had no other choice than to leave town and put the baby up for adoption. Without telling my parents, I zipped up my feelings, put on a set of emotional blinders, and went forward by filling out adoption forms. Then I left for the Bay Area. I had been accepted at University of California–Berkeley for the summer session, and if I maintained a B+ average, I would start in the fall, but by then I had a noticeably pregnant profile, so I postponed my admission for a year.

At my first doctor visit in California, a large ovarian mass was discovered. I was scared, and since I was unable to pay for the necessary surgery, I knew I had to tell my parents. I steeled myself for what they would say. Mom almost hung up on me. Dad was a bit more comforting. I knew I had disappointed them both, but I was more worried about the tumor than about being pregnant. I was afraid it was cancer and that I would die. However, it turned out that the cyst was benign, and the doctor told me I would carry my baby to term.

I was surprised, but grateful, when Mom traveled to California to help me find an apartment where I could live while I waited for my baby to be born. She made me swear not to tell her parents. They'd just die if they knew, she said. You need to look well when you go to Arizona in the spring to visit your grandparents. Walk every day; watch what you eat. I did when I had you. She sounded like a sergeant. I wondered if my birth was difficult for her. As she left my apartment, she glanced over her shoulder and said, No decent man will ever marry you. I felt as if she had whipped me. Too stunned to cry, I grabbed the little kitten I bought to keep me company and held it close as I paced the floor of my shoddy one-room apartment.

In early 1959, I gave birth at the hospital to the baby I named Deborah. On the phone, my mother asked me how it went, and I told her it wasn't too bad. I was glad to have it all behind me now. You're lucky, she said. It took me a long time to have you.

I was too tired to be offended, as if it was my fault it took so long. I was afraid to tell her that I hadn't seen my little girl, only the back of her head as the nurse whisked her out through the delivery-room door. I never got to hold her. The pain of giving her away was so immense that it took me almost forty years to accept my loss and grieve. When the social worker gave me Deb's birth certificate to sign, she said I didn't have to use my own name, but I did, and I put Richard's as well. I refused to lie on an official document.

Returning to college after having the baby wasn't as easy as I expected. I was tired, and my heart ached.

I still wanted to be a doctor, but I'd lost my confidence and settled for a major in psychology instead. The UC campus was about to embrace the Sixties, and I was swept up along with others in demonstrations, sit-ins, and arrests. I didn't have much contact with my parents. I married once, realized my mistake, got divorced, and decided to become a nurse instead of a doctor. Finally, I found Mr. Right—at least I thought so.

In the back of my mind was a little thought: Mark was someone my mother surely couldn't complain about—he was studying to become an Episcopal priest, no less—so I married him.

As the years went by, even when we were living in the same city, Mom and I kept our distance, despite the fact that I had two children, Ethan and Lexa, her grandchildren. We kept in touch every few weeks by phone. I sent her pictures of our children, but often two or three years would pass between our visits. There seemed to be a freeze in our emotional worlds, with no change regardless of the years that passed. I was still nervous when I was around her, and she was still finding fault. Even then I wanted her approval, but as the children got older, I stopped trying. Mark and I were busy raising and enjoying our own family. It was Edith's yearly visits that we looked forward to, rather than any visit with my mother—Edith was still the mother I had had as a child, and we formed a bond that lasted forever.

Preoccupied with scenes from my past, I'd been inching along in the evening commute for more than an hour and almost missed my turnoff. The streetlights turned on as I drove up the hill to our house. I realized that I hadn't lost my mother after all. Mother had entrusted me to Edith when I was still a little girl. It was many years before I understood that Edith's love and centeredness provided the foundation I would need throughout my life. Edith had prepared me to be open to the gift my mother had given me that day. But I wouldn't understand the significance of having two mothers until much later.

Keeping Secrets

Oh what a tangled web we weave, When
first we practice to deceive.

—*Sir Walter Scott*

The acrid smell of burnt coffee filled the air, and strains
from *Graceland* reverberated from our daughter Lexa's
downstairs bedroom. It was at least six-thirty; she was
already awake and getting ready for school when I
heard Mark's heavy footsteps coming down the hall.
He shuffled into our room and plunked a coffee mug
on my bedside table. There was always a bit of anger
in everything he did, but he seemed more prickly than
usual as he walked across the room and jerked back the
curtains. The naked trees stood etched against the pale
Wisconsin morning. I felt apprehensive, but it wasn't
the usual anxiety that had pursued me for years. This
time I was anxious about Mark, not me.

Much later, I understood my outburst, but at the

time, the words that slipped from my mouth seemed to come from nowhere. Are you homosexual? I said in a low voice as I shook off the dream I'd just had.

No!

Then what are you keeping from me?

He looked like a question mark as he stood hunched, immobilized in front of the windows. It's nothing you need to know, he mumbled.

But something's wrong. I *do* need to know. Wrapping my arms around my legs, I rocked back and forth on the bed. Did he want to leave me? I knew he detested my panic attacks—the way they restricted our lives, my always wanting him nearby or available by phone. I never knew when anxiety would seize me, making me feel as though I couldn't breathe.

Nothing I can tell you, he repeated, his voice breaking as he turned his back on me.

You have to. I jumped out of bed and started toward him. He covered his face with his hands.

I stared at him. His thick brown hair was turning gray. His beard was noticeably thin. I was surprised at how tired and old he looked. I heard him say the word addict, but did he say *sexual* addict? What did that mean, I wondered. A few moments later, I heard him mumble something about "hot johns."

What's a hot john? I winced as I said the words.

It's where men go to have sex.

The word AIDS exploded in my head. We had left the Bay Area in 1984. Men there were dying of AIDS. I asked how long he had been doing this.

Since 1975 was his clipped reply.

Had he exposed me to AIDS? I sat back down on the bed, screaming, No one—not you, not anyone—fucks with my life. Do you understand that? I grabbed my pillows and yelled, Make an appointment with the best addiction counselors in the city. We need help. Tell them it's an emergency. I tried to remember from my nursing-school days what to do, whom to contact.

From downstairs, I heard Lexa calling me. Mom, where's my school skirt?

Grabbing my blue tartan robe, I ran down to her room. I left it here last night, I said as I entered her room. Lexa was bopping around in sync with Paul Simon's songs as she brushed her long auburn hair. I watched my beautiful ten-year-old daughter—her world seemingly without worry. What would happen to her if something happened to us? I didn't want her to know how frightened I was. I tried to steady my voice. Have you everything together for classes? I asked. The bus will be here in about thirty minutes.

Yup. All ready. It's just the skirt.

I pointed to the window seat. It's right there, I said. I'm going to get dressed. See you upstairs in a few. Stifling the urge to grab her in my arms, I blew her a kiss instead. We might all have died, I thought as I went upstairs.

At breakfast, in between mouthfuls of cold cereal and frozen raspberries, Lexa chattered away about the school soccer finals that still were to be played. I sat with her at the table, trying to listen, sipping my coffee as though it were just another ordinary day.

I'm through, Mom. Let's go. She pushed away from

the table, and as she did, I looked up and saw Mark leaning against the kitchen doorway, his face twisted, grotesque, like the gargoyles we saw the previous year when we toured the National Cathedral.

Say good-bye to your dad, honey. Then I'll walk you to the bus.

My daughter and I did what we always did— walked down the driveway holding hands, the neighbor's terrier yapping at us as he did every morning. The school bus chattered along the gravel road. I gave Lexa a squeeze before she jumped on the bus. She smelled of cornflakes and the Miss Dior perfume I gave her for her tenth birthday. Don't let anything happen to my girl, I prayed. Don't let anything happen to us.

As I trudged back up to the house, I began to feel weak and shaky. Thoughts whirred through my head. Mark had been betraying me for years. With each step, my anger grew. Should I tell him to leave?

Mark was sitting at the table reading the paper as I entered the kitchen. The four of us had always had our breakfasts together there before our son, Ethan, went away to boarding school. It was hard to believe that it was 1987 now. Lexa was in fifth grade, and Ethan was in his first year of college. He would be coming home for the Christmas holidays and would sense immediately that something was wrong between his dad and me. He needed to be told. I wasn't going to hide our confrontation from him, and I didn't want to face this problem alone. But I couldn't tell Lexa. She was too young. I wanted to protect her.

Scared to talk to Mark, I stared out the bay windows

at the nature lake behind the house. I noticed that the water had frozen overnight. The Canada geese had already flown south, and the maples and oaks were naked, leaving only the evergreens to withstand the fast-approaching winter.

As I poured my coffee, I thought about how it happened that we'd had to leave our California home in 1982, five years earlier. I felt a shiver go through me, as if I knew something I shouldn't know. We had been living close to my parents' winter home, near the Pacific Ocean. Mark had put aside his medical practice after being hired to be both chaplain and English teacher at the nearby Episcopal day school. He had never taught school before, but he turned out to be a natural and was a hit with both the children and their parents. And then, three years into his job—without any warning or formal complaint—the contract he had signed the previous week was withdrawn. The headmistress demanded his resignation. At the time, I wondered why the diocesan bishop, the board of trustees, and the local Episcopal rector were all present when he was dismissed. I thought it was strange that I was the only board member who hadn't been notified to attend the meeting. A few weeks later, one of the board members, a close friend of my mom's, took me to lunch and advised me to resign. She hinted that it would be easier on my mother if I did. Mom had been widowed for only a year.

As I walked across the room and sat down at the table, I began to wonder. Did his dismissal have anything to do with what he'd just disclosed? I watched as he ran his fingers over the veins on the back of his hand, a habit he'd had since medical school. I knew how testy and belligerent he could be when cornered. I'd have to approach him cautiously, as if he were an agitated patient.

What have you done to us, I whispered as I sat down in front of him. Will you explain what's been going on? You said this problem started in 1975, right?

He remained silent and looked at me with sad, smoky-blue eyes. You'd better help me with this, God, because I don't know what to do. I swallowed hard and started again. Please, can you tell me…what is a sex addict?

Read Carnes's book *Out of the Shadows*. It's all in there, I thought I heard him mumble.

I'd never heard of the book or what he was referring to. Just tell me what's going on, Mark. What are we facing? I imagined a hospital ward full of AIDS patients wasting away, dying. Surely he wouldn't have endangered himself. After all, he was a physician. He knew the dangers. What exactly have you been doing? I said.

Acting out.

Acting out? You mean you've been going to those places for twelve years? That's over half our married life together! I felt I was drowning as the words "twelve years" rolled over me. Did he mean twelve years of occasional liaisons, or did he mean continuous contacts during the time we were trying to conceive a child? Perhaps that was that why it took me so long to get pregnant the second time.

We sat in silence while I scrambled to absorb the implications of what he said. The only sound in the kitchen was the cuckoo clock. Like a time bomb, it ticked loudly from across the room. I was desperate to know everything. Leaning forward, I pinched out the words. What exactly do you mean by acting out? I said.

He began by explaining that he went to johns and mutually masturbated with men. I tried to absorb this idea. I felt a sharp pain in my stomach, as though a knife had pierced me. Terrified, I jumped up from my chair, ready to hit him. I shouted instead. Why do you hate me so much? You've risked our lives and our kids'.

Ducking his head, he pushed himself away from the table. I *don't* hate you, he snapped.

But people don't do things like that to people they love.

He didn't look at me but focused intently on our corgi instead, who by now was standing at attention by his feet.

It was hard for me to believe that my husband—a physician and an Episcopal priest—had been gambling with my life and cheating on me for all those years. What are we going to do? I said. I felt dizzy and quickly sat down.

I don't know. You have every right to tell me to leave.

Leave, I thought. But if he left, how would I manage my ever-present anxiety and panic attacks? I was too angry at the time to notice that in that very moment of crisis I wasn't having an anxiety attack. I couldn't see my own strength. Instead, I focused on whether I could raise Lexa alone. I remembered 1973. Mark and I divorced for six months. Ethan was only five at the time. I didn't like being a single parent then, and I didn't think I'd like it any better now. Did Mark want to leave me? Was he really an addict? Was addiction an illness or a choice? What about our marital vows? Should I stay with him? Could I help him heal this thing, whatever it was?

I knew he'd been seeing a spiritual counselor for three years, a former Roman Catholic priest who had left the church, married, and was now a psychologist.

So you and your doctor have been keeping this secret from me all this time? Didn't either of you ever consider that you were putting my life in danger? You could have killed Lexa before she was born! What were the two of you thinking?

Mark got up and headed for the hallway. I followed him. He wasn't going to get away from me. I needed to hear the whole story. Darting in front of him, I put my hands out to stop him and said, Tell me how this started. Please, tell me what happened. I'll try to understand.

He ambled back to the kitchen, and we took our places again at the table. He spoke in a small, lifeless voice. He said that he began going to johns shortly after we returned to the Bay Area in 1975. He saw a man masturbating in the university gym, and he was hooked. He had to go back again. I asked him how many times. He said he'd been a lot, and then I asked him if he'd been tested for AIDS.

He fired his answer across the table. No.

Why not?

Because I'm not at risk.

I asked if he masturbated only himself or if they did it to each other.

Both, he said.

You know you're at risk, I said. You have sores on your hands from your dermatitis. You need to get tested.

I'll give it some thought. He tossed his head in that arrogant manner he had.

I felt empty and cold. I was scared to death that I'd been exposed to AIDS.

The phone rang—probably the counselor returning Mark's earlier phone call. I told him to answer the phone downstairs in his den. I needed a break.

Gazing around the kitchen, I saw memories of our life together, photos of our children and friends, a wooden boat sculpture, several colorful glazed pots. As I poured myself another cup of coffee, I thought about Mark's betrayal. I wanted to hide from the world. I knew right then that there wasn't any way a counselor could help us. The trust between us was broken, and we would never be the same again.

Suddenly, Mark appeared at the kitchen door, holding his glasses in his hand. His eyes were fixed, his face motionless. I noticed he hadn't put on a clean shirt that morning, and he'd forgotten to put on his belt. He said we had an appointment the next morning with Dr. Anthony Taylor, a psychologist who worked with addictions.

A shiver went through me, and I wrapped my sweater tightly around my shoulders and continued to press him with more questions: where had he done these things; did he have oral or anal sex?

No, he said.

Could I believe what he told me? I wondered if this was how we would end our marriage, in the kitchen, talking about his sex life, while the clock ticked away in the background. I shook my head in disbelief and said, Mark, we're talking about your life here, our children, my life, and our life together. You've jeopardized all that. Do you understand?

Yes to all of that, he mumbled.

I felt the contempt in his voice as I remembered the time he had chastised me in front of our children, making me tell them how much my anxieties had crippled my life. It was approaching noon. By then, I'd learned that everywhere we lived, he had been in men's rooms: shopping malls, bookstores, performance halls, and universities. I remembered the time we were in Saks. Lexa was with us—she was only two. It was 1979. Mark bought me a stunning black-velvet bathrobe. It was covered with Georgia O'Keefe–style flowers, spectacular orange-pink camellias with huge, sweeping green leaves. I had worn it every Christmas since then. Did you go to one of those places when you were buying me my Christmas robe? I asked.

He answered first with silence, followed by a slow, agonizing yes.

I grabbed the edge of the table and said, Who the hell do you think you are? He didn't answer.

Much later, I would discover that he called himself a chameleon.

We sat through a painful silence, and then he told me he'd been caught in a department-store bathroom by in-house security. He said he'd wanted to confess to me earlier but was afraid to. For a moment I withdrew, trying to imagine what the headlines in the local paper would have been if he'd gone to jail. My mother would have seen them.

You have to stop now, I said. This can't happen again. Not ever.

Exhausted after a morning of grilling, and wanting to put some space between us, I got up from the table and walked slowly by the sliding doors to our deck. I glanced out the window at the winter pasture where my long-eared Nubian goats were grazing. They were reminders of carefree times, the 4-H project Ethan and I did together when we lived in the California valley.

I looked across the room at Mark and asked, How will I be able to trust you? I'll always be wondering if you're in a "hot john," as you call it. Not waiting for his reply, I cringed as I asked him one more question: While we've been living here in Madison, when did you go to these places?

On the way to see my therapist.

Could I believe what I heard? Mark quickly added that his therapist thought he was suicidal. As I grappled with that possibility, I asked him why his therapist didn't have him hospitalized.

I'm tired of answering your questions, he said. I've

told you everything. I'm tired of your anger. He stood up and marched out of the room.

That's too bad, I snapped after him. If you didn't want me to be angry, you shouldn't have done what you did.

We spoke in monosyllables during dinner, while Lexa eagerly described the day's soccer game and then chattered about what she was planning for her science project. Mark cleared the table and left for his den. I was alone in the kitchen thinking, what next? I needed to get out of the house and away from Mark. I ached all over and couldn't think clearly.

Lexa was in her room studying German for the next day when I told her I was going over to a friend's for a short while. I whispered in her ear, I'll be back before you're ready for bed. I love you so much.

She looked up at me with her hazel-brown eyes and smiled. I love you, too, Mom.

Filled with fear, I wondered what would happen to my precious girl. What would happen to our son, to us? I gave her a quick hug and left the room.

I got into my car and drove out onto the country road and into the darkness. I felt fouled and contaminated. Every time Mark had been with someone else, he had violated me. My legs began to shake uncontrollably, and I pulled over to the side of the road. I couldn't see any headlights coming in either direction. From deep within me I yelled, God, where are you? Help me. I don't know what to do! I pounded on the steering wheel until my hands burned. I didn't know how much time had passed as I sat trying to sort out all the whirling images and unwelcome truths. The hardest part was that I believed what Mark had told me. I knew it had to be true, all of it, and I was frightened. Suddenly I felt terribly alone.

When I arrived home, I went downstairs to Lexa's room and quietly opened her door and asked, Are you still awake, Lexa?

Yup. She sat up in bed.

I just wanted to say good night. Remember always, I love you, no matter what. I kissed her on the forehead, and she snuggled under the covers. I tucked a favorite bear in bed beside her, the pink and white one I'd made her eight years ago, when she was two.

I shuddered as I walked upstairs to my room. Mark had to be tested for AIDS. So did I. Even the thought of it made me gag. Leaving my clothes in a pile on the floor, I slipped into my nightgown and crawled into bed. What would the therapist say tomorrow? Did I help create this nightmare?

I must have fallen asleep. The next thing I knew, Mark was getting into bed. I sat up abruptly and stared at him. What are you doing here? I snapped.

I'm going to bed, he said, yanking back the covers.

Maybe you are, but not in this bed. Go to Ethan's or the guest room.

No, I want to sleep in my own bed.

I grabbed my pillows and started toward the door, Where are you going?

Somewhere where you and your men friends are not. I left the room and hurried downstairs to the family room. I tried to get comfortable on the couch.

I had never deliberately left our bed in anger before. Aunt Ellen's words rang in my ears. Before we were married, I took Mark to meet her. She walked me to her bedroom and looked me straight in the eye. It's important: never go to bed angry. You'll have disagreements, but when you go to bed, hug one another. You never know what the next day will bring.

Her words haunted me now. But Mark didn't like to be hugged. He said it was because he hadn't grown up in a family that showed affection.

The sofa sagged in the middle. I missed my own bed. My mind flooded with memories, and I couldn't sleep. The first few years had been good. Then came the stresses of parenthood, coupled with graduate school for both of us. My anxieties kicked in as well. The distance between us was magnified and grew harder to ignore.

Throughout that dismal night on the couch, as I visited and revisited scenes and conversations, I remembered the dream I had that morning. Quickly I reached for some paper and grabbed a pen from the coffee table. I scrunched myself in the corner of the sofa and began to write what I recalled.

In the distance, a volcano erupted. Its bright red lava flow pierced the darkness as it surged down the mountainside. I was at the dude ranch where we went for spring vacation. I wanted to show a friend the exquisitely plumed bird I'd found. It had a crown of feathers gleaming with desert pinks and gold and a long tail, resembling a peacock. As we walked, we saw an old woman stumbling along the road. Her forbidding dream face, deeply lined with wrinkles and conveying confusion, lingered before my eyes. I sensed Mark was missing. I searched for him and found him sitting in a long, narrow adobe room. It smelled of leather and was lined with books. He was reading in the dark. I turned on the lamp beside him. He didn't move. I turned off the light and left him in the shadows.

Leaning back into the sofa pillows, I reviewed my dream. I worked through it the way I used to do in seminars when years ago I had attended the Gestalt Institute. By morning I was clear: if I wanted to understand how this heartbreak had occurred, I would need to follow the threads back through our marriage and before.

3

Memories of Mark

Bless O Lord, this Ring, that he who gives it
and she who wears it may abide in thy peace,
and continue in thy favour, unto their life's
end; through Jesus Christ our Lord. Amen
—*Book of Common Prayer, 1928*

It all began in mid-October 1964 during the eleven
o'clock Sunday service in Grace Cathedral, San Francisco. Someone behind me reached forward and
tapped me on the shoulder. I looked around and was
surprised to see Ann, a classmate from the New York
boarding school I had attended for five years. I hadn't
seen her since we'd graduated eight years earlier. She
hadn't changed a bit—still blonde, tall, and sporting
a smile. As we chatted during coffee hour, I learned
that Ann and her husband, John, an Episcopal priest,
had recently moved to San Francisco. She invited me to
dinner the following Saturday.

When I arrived at their condo, John handed me a glass of cold white wine. As we began to visit, a little girl with flaxen hair, wearing a bright pink tutu and striped orange socks, ran giggling to her father and peeked at me from behind his legs.

This is Sally. She's just turned three—still a bit shy. John scooped her up in his arms, and I smiled at her. Ann and John were both from the East Coast. Like most of my classmates, Ann married shortly after college and had already started her family. As I sipped my wine and leaned into their luxurious leather couch, I was feeling slightly out of place. I was in my first year of nursing school at the University of California, San Francisco Medical Center, getting a second degree, unmarried, and not accustomed to dinner parties. It was hard to unwind from a week on pediatrics caring for terminally ill children, one of whom had died earlier that day. Being around little children reminded me of the baby I had given away. Deborah was the secret I had kept since I was nineteen.

We invited a friend of John's to join us tonight, Ann announced cheerfully as she placed a plate of cocktail crackers, cream cheese, and smoked salmon on the coffee table. He's in his last year of seminary—he'll graduate this spring, in May.

I tried to hide the disappointment on my face. How nice of you. I wished she'd asked me if I wanted a blind date, but I was too polite to say so.

As if reading my mind, Ann went on. Mark and John grew up together. They lost touch when they went to college, but they met again when we were in Idaho.

John had a small parish. Mark filled in as a seminarian when some of the clergy were on vacation.

Cripes, not a man who was headed for the priesthood. And certainly not one who had been hanging out in Idaho. This was going to be one dull evening.

John was fixing drinks when the doorbell rang. In walked an attractive man wearing an expensive tweed sports jacket and gray flannels. He held his hand out to John. Under his arm, he carried an LP recording. May I help you with those drinks, mister? He gave a practiced smile. Mark had brown hair, a full oval face, and an air of affluence.

I was just getting it ready. John handed Mark an old-fashioned, adding, How's it going across the Bay?

Basically well. Only seven months to go. He raised his glass and took a long drink. He didn't seem like a seminarian to me. He looked more like a third-year law student headed for a big firm than a future priest.

Mark walked quickly to the couch and put his drink on the table next to my wine glass. He placed his record beside it and ran his long fingers over the colorful cover. I'm Mark. How do you know Ann and John?

His hands were smooth, no trace of any scars— they'd never seen hard labor—but the cuffs of his oxford shirt were worn. I felt his blue eyes penetrating me. He grinned, and I noticed a wink—or was it a nervous tic? I settled in for lively conversation, thinking maybe it wouldn't be such a tedious evening after all.

We soon learned that we had both attended colleges on the East Coast. We had even gone to the same religious conference in the Pocono Mountains when we were in high school, and we tried to remember if we had met. I admitted I hadn't enjoyed the weekend very much and spent most of my time ice-skating.

You wouldn't have seen me on the ice. I never learned to skate, but I lettered in track when I was in college, he said quickly.

Intriguing, but I didn't think he was doing much running now. From the looks of his waistline, he'd put on some weight after college. I mentioned the record album he brought, Leontyne Price singing in *Il Travatore*, and discovered that we both enjoyed opera and classical music.

I don't remember much of the dinner. I was mostly interested in what Mark had to say. I wanted to appear knowledgeable as the two men debated the merits of situation ethics, a hot theological topic.

As the evening went on, I thought I could like this man. Ann and John must have sneaked off to the kitchen. I barely heard their voices. Matchmakers! We sat together in their living room, prolonging our conversation. Mark captivated me. He spoke easily about his interests: English literature, music—he confessed to having a good bass voice and being attracted to the theater. I watched him closely. He seemed a little stilted, removed a bit, being someone he wasn't, like an actor. He chose his words precisely and delivered them with just a touch of emphasis, as though...Of course, as a seminarian he was probably used to giving sermons, used to being in front of people.

A few hours later, with Ann and John popping in

and out of the living room—checking on us, I was sure—the evening ended, and Mark walked me to my car. He leaned toward me, taking his time before he asked me if I'd like to go to dinner and a movie the next Saturday. I shivered, not with cold, but with a rush of emotion. I tried to hide my excitement as I accepted his invitation.

I'll pick you up about six-thirty, then?

But not unless you have my address and phone number, I said, jotting them on a scrap of paper. I handed it to him with my best smile.

That's great. See you next Saturday. Gracefully, he stepped back from my car. I waved at him and drove off humming, Hello, young lovers...what was I singing? I didn't even know his last name! I'd had my share of dates in my life, but this man seemed different, even a bit mysterious. I thought he had the right mixture of assurance and tenderness. I could do without the crew cut, but I liked the leather patches on the elbows of his sports coat. He fascinated me.

The next seven days crawled by. I thought about Mark constantly, picturing him studying or standing in front of a congregation. I drew scenes around him: picking me up for our date, walking with him on a beach. What did he look like underneath those Easterner clothes he wore? Was he really bright? Could he be funny? Could he love me?

Finally, it was Saturday afternoon. I'd spent the week trying to decide what to wear. I didn't want to overdress. As I stood in front of the mirror in my San Francisco apartment, my hazel eyes laughed back at me. My light-green eye shadow made my eyes look larger, and I thought I looked pretty as I brushed my shoulder-length brown hair away from my face. I tried out various expressions in the mirror: positive, engrossed, surprised, and kind. I smiled to bring out my dimples—they were one of my best features. I didn't have a bad figure, either. I pinched my cheeks and reached for my pink-tinted lipstick. What perfume to wear? Caron's Bellodgia, spicy floral, slightly dark, my favorite; a drop behind each ear, a drop on each wrist, and I was ready.

Promptly at six-thirty, the doorbell rang. I almost ran to the door. Slow down, I told myself, trying to contain my excitement. There he stood in a navy-blue blazer and dark gray slacks, a bashful smile on his face. He thrust a bouquet of pale peach roses toward me. Butterflies tickled my stomach. His hand brushed mine as he handed me the flowers, and I felt electricity crackle between us.

They're exquisite, I said. Please, come inside. Would you like a glass of wine? I'll be just a minute. I want to put these in a vase, I said, rushing to the kitchenette.

Wine would be fine, red or white. He sat on the couch. Don't hurry. Mind if I look at your library?

Oh no, go right ahead. I'd hardly call it a library, but I do like to read. Silly girl, I thought, of course you like to read. But I didn't want him to think I was some sort of bookworm.

He wandered over to the bookcase. So do I, but there's not much time for anything but studying while I'm in seminary, he said.

Same here: pharmacology, psychology, nursing procedures, and lots of hours in the field. Not much time left over for Wordsworth or Cummings. I held out a tray with glasses of white wine and roasted almonds.

You like Cummings? he asked, as he pulled my big book of poetry off the top shelf. Have a seat. I'll read a special one for you. He flipped to a page and began to read. "Somewhere I have never traveled, gladly beyond." He read all but the last line and then closed the book. Looking at me he recited, "Nobody, not even the rain, has such small hands." His eyes were glistening, and his face held both a question and an answer. I'd have to wait until he asked the question before I'd give an answer, but I was delighted he had read me a love poem.

We lingered over our dinner at a less-than-glamorous restaurant in the East Bay, where we ordered sauerkraut, beef brisket, and beer. It was crowded and noisy, a poor choice for a first date. Not a bit romantic. I wondered why he chose it. Maybe he was testing me.

As he spoke, he painted word pictures of the time he spent in South Africa with a Christian youth group. I visualized the green hills and valleys and the brightly colored clothing that the women wore. Later, when I saw his photographs, I knew he was gifted with a camera. His deep, liquid voice turned me on.

I like hearing you talk about where you've been, I said. It's like being there with you. The words tumbled out of my mouth, and he listened to me carefully. Eager to share our thoughts and our lives, we talked about

our families, civil rights, JFK, and Vietnam. Toward the
end of dinner, he took my hand and held it. My entire
body blushed.

Earlier, we had decided to see a forgettable art
movie that I no longer remember. He bought a box
of mint chocolates and made love to my hand as we
watched the film. A few hours later, we pulled up in
front of my apartment. With his arm around my waist,
he walked me to the front porch. Would he want to
come inside? I put my key in the lock.

Wait a minute. He pulled me to him and held me
tightly, and then he placed his lips on mine. His kiss
startled me. He was firm and demanding. I wanted
him to hold me forever. I leaned into him; aroused, he
pressed himself against me. Seconds later we stepped
away.

Tomorrow, he said. Would you like to go across the
bridge and have a picnic at one of the wineries? It may
be cold.

You can keep me warm. I laughed. But then I
stopped abruptly as I saw a slight wrinkle sneak across
his forehead. Oops. Episcopal priest. Better be more
reserved. Just kidding, I said. I'll bring a heavy jacket.
Want me to fix us a picnic? I asked, watching his face
relax.

Certainly, and we can buy some wine when we're
there. He reached for me again. He was like a little boy
playing peek-a-boo, one moment engaged, the next
gone. He squeezed me tightly, almost too hard for a
hug, and then pulled away with a big grin. Good night,
Sweet Gale.

I blew him a kiss as he stepped into his car. My cheeks felt warm, and there was an irreverent tingling in my stomach. I felt special being called Sweet Gale.

That fall we spent all our free time together wandering through the city, riding cable cars, sampling restaurants, and going to the opera and symphony. I filled my lungs with salty ocean air and smelled sweet chocolate from Ghirardelli Square. We roamed the beaches north of the Golden Gate Bridge and drove through the fragrant eucalyptus groves in the North Bay hills. We shared our favorite sites with one another and made new memories—finding places neither of us had been before. I thought it strange that he never took my hand as we walked together, peering in the various shop windows. I let him drive my little yellow Porsche, which my dad gave me when I graduated from UC Berkeley. I introduced him to my friends. I felt the sun was shining just for me, and I was showing off, so pleased with myself for having found this bright and sensitive man to love. I felt beautiful and cherished. When I wasn't with Mark, I was thinking about him—imagining what it would be like to be his wife.

One night, about a month after we'd started to date, Mark asked me to join him for dinner at the seminary. I told him I'd be on a clinical assignment, and I wouldn't have time to change from my uniform. He said he didn't mind and to come as I was. I think he wanted to see what I looked like when dressed as a student nurse in my blue-and-white-striped uniform. I followed him into the large dining room. It was a rowdy meal, more like a fraternity than a seminary.

After dinner, he walked me to his dorm. He had a single room with books all over, messy student style.

I'm just memorizing vocabulary for Greek tomorrow, he said. You can use the desk if you'd like. He dropped down on his bed and stretched out his legs. I wasn't a neatnik myself, so that worked, but I didn't know what to think of the small songbirds chirping in their cage. They had intriguing markings, mostly earth colors. They could sing, but I preferred furry animals— cats, mostly, and dogs. We'd work out something in the future.

Spreading out my pharmacology text, I tried to concentrate. A half-hour must have passed when I sensed he was staring at me. I looked up to see a silly grin on his face. What are you thinking about?

I'm thinking about asking you to marry me.

Oh, really? I turned back to my book and smoothed the page, which blurred in front of me.

Well, will you? He raised his eyebrows in anticipation.

Jumping up, I ran into his outstretched arms. Yes, Mark. Of course I'll marry you!

He was trembling as we embraced. Blowing softly in my ear, he said, Married.

Yes, really married. I leaned back and looked up at him. I saw a tiny muscle tremble just below his left eye. I touched his face, running my fingers over his lips.

I'd like John to be a groomsman, he said, stepping to one side, almost as if inspecting me.

His grandfather and mine were in each other's weddings.

Perfect. And Ann can be my matron of honor. I took a deep breath. When do you want to do this?

As soon as I graduate this coming spring.

I was delighted. We talked late into the evening, planning our wedding together. I wanted to be married in Grace Cathedral and to have Bishop Pike perform the ceremony. It was my parish home. I'd been confirmed there two years earlier, and now I was the Sunday school director. Mark wanted to arrange the music. The date and our decisions about members of the wedding party were my biggest concerns. I figured the rest of it was food and colors.

I began to choke up and feel all wobbly inside. Just hug me, will you? He held me, and we began a slow dance.

When our heartbeats slowed down, he said he needed to ask my father for my hand. I appreciated the respect he showed me. It was one of the things I loved about him. I felt giddy. A married lady—I was going to be a married lady! A small thought occurred to me: my mother would have to approve of me now, but I wasn't going to worry about that just yet.

We leaned back on the pillows. I ran my fingers through his hair. I have to drive back across the Bay tonight, I said. I don't think I can stay here.

You're right. That wouldn't work. One more kiss, then we can go down to your car.

We held each other and kissed for a long time. I snuggled against his chest, feeling safe, warm, and sexy until it really was time to leave.

He came to my apartment the next night for dinner

and presented me with an elegant Japanese arrangement of flowers. How considerate he was, sometimes almost to the point of being formal. I hesitated for a moment, wondering why, and then realized that his doing so made me feel valued.

How many women have you been in love with? I stood behind his chair, trailing my fingertips over the back of his neck.

None. He stood up. There was a hint of added color in his face.

No one?

Not anyone. I dated a girl when I was in college, but we were only good friends. It was never a love affair. He seemed a bit defensive. I just wanted to know who'd come before me. There weren't any others, he added. I went to debutante parties and dated a little, but I never fell in love with anyone.

Then why me?

I was sure about you as soon as I met you at Ann and John's that night for supper. I knew I was going to ask you to marry me. I went back to seminary that night and walked into Jack's room. I told him, I've just met the girl I'm going to marry.

You knew? When had I known? Probably when I saw his hands on his record album. Something about his hands intrigued me. Strong, yet gentle.

He put an arm around me and pulled me closer to him. Slowly at first, as though the sun were just rising, a glow inside me began to spread.

Now what, I said as I nestled my head against his neck.

What do you mean, now what?

Well, we're engaged. We're going to be married in five months. Don't you think maybe?

He sounded alarmed. Maybe what?

That maybe we could make love. We'd better find out how we do in bed too. I was trying to tease him. I wanted to tell him to lighten up.

He didn't answer at first. Had I been too forward? Perhaps I should have let him make the first move, but I had thought that was where things were going as we held one another. When he spoke again, it was with considerable reluctance. He told me he'd never made love to anyone. That surprised me—he was twenty-six—but his hesitation was understandable. I wasn't going to tell him about my experience just yet, so was I seducing him? I wasn't certain. I held out my hand and led him upstairs to my bedroom.

Make yourself comfortable. I'm just going to slip into the bathroom for a minute. I felt along the top shelf of my cupboard for my diaphragm. I hoped he'd gotten some of his clothes off. I filled the little cup with jelly. When I returned, Mark was looking out the window. Did he expect me to be a virgin? It didn't matter—I wasn't—and right now, that seemed to be a good thing. Mark looked down at the rug, avoiding my eyes. I waited for him to make a move toward me. When he didn't, I lay down on my bed and said, Come here, Mark. I reached out my hand to him. He walked toward me and then, almost falling onto the bed and me, he held me gently and began to kiss me, slowly at first and then with excitement.

Despite his inexperience, he seemed to know what to do. We moved in rhythm with one another. Not bad for a first time.

I stroked Mark's face and felt sweat at the fringe of his temples. He rolled over on his back, both of us spent.

Hmm, I just want to stay here forever, he whispered.

It will be forever. Just not all-at-once forever.

Two months later, Mark took me to an expensive East Indian restaurant on Nob Hill. He'd been secretive of late and somewhat shy, a side of him I hadn't seen before. After we ordered our drinks, he pulled a small black-velvet box out of his breast pocket and grinned as he pushed it in my direction. Open it, he said.

Now I had to tell him. I took a deep breath as a shiver ran through my body. I have two things I want you to know before I open it, I said. He raised his eyebrows in surprise. I continued to speak before he could tell me to stop. My father is manic-depressive. I want you to know that. He has ups and downs sometimes. Mark folded his hands together on the table and leaned forward. One other thing: I had a baby girl. I placed her up for adoption. I told my parents what had happened. I told her father that he and I were both too young to be married and too young to have a family. My voice quivered as I added, I will understand if you don't want to marry me. I know I'm considered used goods.

Neither of those things makes any difference to me, he said in a clear voice. I love you.

The following spring we were married in San Francisco. I was the first bride to walk through Grace Cathedral's new doors, replicas of Ghiberti's bronze *Gates of Paradise* in Florence. They shimmered in the warm morning sun. Mark arranged for a trumpeter to play "The Trumpet Shall Sound" from Handel's *Messiah*.

As I took my father's arm, he whispered, You know I don't usually go to church. But for you, I'd waltz down the aisle. Dad patted my gloved hand and said, Don't forget to smile. Hold tight. Here we go.

The rows of standing guests moved by me like ocean waves. I felt almost sick with excitement. As we approached the transept of the church, I saw the white gardenias on my mother's black straw hat. I thought to myself, See what I've done now, Mom? I've got me a priest.

For a second, as Dad stepped back to leave me at the altar, I felt a sudden flash of panic, but Mark reached into his pocket and pulled out a spray bottle of decongestant I used when I had a cold. He'd teased me about my breathing, saying all I needed was a squirt. Now he winked and put it back into his pocket. Swallowing a giggle, I relaxed, and the service began. My attendants, wearing moss-green dresses, carried baskets filled with roses, freesia, and daffodils. Mark had designed my bouquet, three sprays of ivory cymbidiums intertwined with ivy.

I told Bishop Pike to speak the service, not to sing it—he had a whiskey voice—but true to form, he broke into a liturgical chant. I glanced at Mark. He rolled his eyes and gave me a wink as the ceremony continued. I thought it would never end. Just before we started our vows, I heard the clang of the cable cars as they

trundled down Sacramento Street. We knelt before
the altar; Bishop Pike took off his clerical stole and
wrapped it tightly around our outstretched hands.
Those whom God has joined together let no man put
asunder. His words echoed off the stone walls.

Putting his hand under my elbow, Mark helped
me to my feet. A few seconds later I heard the bishop
say, You may kiss the bride. I turned toward Mark. He
winked at me again and placed a delicate kiss on my
lips. I was relieved and excited. I'd done it: I'd married
a respectable man.

We turned and waved to the congregation. The
organ burst forth with the majestic Widor *Toccata in D
Minor* as we raced down the aisle out into the brilliant
sunshine. Together with the bishop, we stood in front
of the cathedral. It was then that I noticed the bishop's
loafers didn't match. One was black, the other brown.
I laughed out loud, and the photographer caught my
smile in his lens.

A luncheon reception was held at a San Francisco
landmark, the Mark Hopkins Hotel. We visited with
friends, danced, sang, and told stories late into the
afternoon. My mother pulled me aside to tell me that
my mother-in-law was tiring and so I needed to throw
my bouquet and get on my way. With "Just Married"
attached to the rear of the yellow Porsche, we drove
across the Golden Gate Bridge for our weekend honeymoon. I had to be back in class on Monday morning.

Mark arranged for our bed at the inn to be covered
with gardenias, my favorite fragrant flower. As we
replayed our glorious day over a gourmet dinner by

the Bay, I asked him why he'd taken me to that taste-
less little restaurant on our first date. He grinned as
he explained that he wanted to see my reaction. Well,
what was it?

It didn't seem to faze you. He paused. So I knew
that you could handle the bumps.

Looking back on it now, I realize that maybe I had
handled those moments *too* well. Perhaps that was
why it took me years to understand how it all went so
wrong.

4

After the Wedding

Bliss it was that dawn to be alive, But to be
young was very heaven.
> —*William Wadsworth*

Are you watching him, whispered Mark. He's actually
looking around. Ethan had arrived quickly, just in
time to be a tax deduction near the end of 1967. Mark
sat next to me in the postdelivery room, holding our
newborn son in his arms.

I don't think he can focus very well just yet, Mark.
I tried rolling over on my side to watch the two of
them. It was an easy delivery, no anesthesia. I held
out my arms. Let me hold him. I need to nurse him if
he's hungry. I held my hand firmly against his small,
downy head and pushed his face to my breast. I don't
know how to do this, but I hope he knows what to do.
Ow-wee! That feels funny, kind of a hard tickle. He
must be sucking.

All the equipment seems to be working. Mark grinned and leaned back in the vinyl-covered hospital chair.

Yes. Oh no. Now he's stopped. His eyes are shut. I touched his tiny nose.

Maybe he's sleepy after his journey. I think he looks like your great uncle.

He doesn't look like anybody, Mark. Not yet. It's too early. I pulled at the pale-blue hospital blanket Ethan was wrapped in. I want to see his toes. I counted each one. They're perfect, I announced. Everything about him is perfect.

Mark leaned over and kissed us both. Thank you.

You're welcome, I said softly, as I held our miracle in my arms.

Six months later, just before July 4, Mark drove us across the Bay Bridge and headed east. I was already missing the conversations I had enjoyed with my friend Lara as we strolled in Golden Gate Park with our new babies. Certainly, it was a new adventure to go to Ohio, where Mark would attend medical school, but I wondered if we would ever return to the elegant City by the Bay. Ethan's portable crib was snug behind the front seats, right next to his father's caged songbirds. By the end of our second day out, he was crying and the birds were screeching. While I drove, Mark resorted to bouncing Ethan on his knee, singing "Raindrops keep falling on my head." It sounded like wishful thinking as we sweated in muggy ninety-degree weather. The air conditioner had conked out on the first day of our four-day trip to the Midwest.

As we approached Ohio, we were surprised to hear on the radio that rioting had broken out in Glenville. We would be living in Elmwood Heights, and we didn't know how far we were from the riots. Keeping the radio tuned to the news, we soon learned that the mayor had called in the National Guard. I remembered two summers before, in '65, when Watts erupted in anger over police brutality and racial discrimination. I wondered how different things might have been if Dr. King and Bobby Kennedy hadn't been gunned down earlier that year.

I felt uneasy as Mark drove up the driveway to the home we'd bought, worried that the unrest might spread throughout the city. Hugging Ethan close to me, I stared at the house. It seemed larger than I remembered. The neighborhood was manicured and somber, hardly like the Haight-Ashbury district in San Francisco where we had rented a stucco bungalow. I was used to the shabby chic of San Francisco and wasn't at all sure I would like Elmwood Heights. What if I couldn't manage the house, our baby, and my role as wife of a priest and future physician? Pushing aside my apprehension, I unpacked and we settled in, starting our new life as a medical-student's family.

Like all medical students in training, Mark's days were long. My anxiety only worsened with his absence. I felt deserted in the huge house with only Ethan. My loneliness morphed into long stretches of exhaustion and worry. Often I awoke feeling I couldn't breathe and afraid I was dying. I was grateful for the days when Mark was able to spend time feeding Ethan before leaving at seven. After he left, I'd be on my own again, taking care of Ethan and trying to fend off my mounting fears as best I could.

One morning early in October, I saw dark clouds threatening rain again. I didn't see how I could get through one more day alone. My throat tightened as I tried to swallow. I kept telling myself I wouldn't be anxious today. Ethan and I will play, and then we'll...I had no idea how to control the waves of discomfort and dread. If only Mark could stay with me. I pulled on my jeans and sweatshirt and splashed my face with cold water. Starting down the stairs, I felt dizzy and flushed. I called out for Mark, but my own voice echoed in the hallway. I walked into the kitchen with a smile appliquéd on my face. Do you have to go in so early today? I said.

God, I hated myself when I said that, being dependent on Mark all the time, feeling like a coward, ashamed and small. I forced a little laugh as I watched Ethan playing with his cereal and glanced at the kitchen clock. Mark would be leaving any minute. The doorbell rang, announcing that his ride was here. I lifted Ethan and swung him onto my hip. Suddenly my head was whirring; I couldn't catch my breath. Mark, I'm scared. Please hold me, talk to me. Don't leave.

Stop it, Gale. I have to go now. He paused to give me a quick hug. He was as rigid as a bronze statue.

I'm trying. I clutched Ethan in my arms. Will you call before you start class?

If I can. His back was already turned. Without another word, he walked out the door.

I'd seen the sadness and frustration in Mark's eyes when he hugged me. I knew he loved me, but I also knew that he hated it when I couldn't control my anxiety attacks. We avoided talking about "my problem," but no matter what I tried, I continued to have terrifying feelings that I couldn't breathe and was going to die.

As I put Ethan in his crib for his afternoon nap that day, I decided to hire someone to care for him while I got a part-time job. I heard there was a mental-health center nearby that was looking for nursing staff, and I wondered if I could find a job there. I really needed to get out of the house and make some friends. I hired Omi, as we came to call her, through an employment agency. She became like a grandmother to Ethan, baking him scrumptious German-chocolate cake with fudge frosting for his birthdays. She was easy to be around and full of energy. She told me to go about my job while she took care of Ethan, the house, and even the shopping. I was so relieved to have her help.

Within a week, I had a job as the only nurse on the three-to-eleven evening shift at the nearby mental-health center. I had hoped that taking the position would take my mind off my anxiety, but it didn't. Then, without much thought, I told Mark I had decided to return to graduate school, a plan I had before we left California. It would take me two years to acquire a master's degree in psychiatric nursing. I would graduate in the spring of 1971.

Before starting classes, I screwed up my courage and sought a doctor's opinion about my attacks. After I explained the nervousness I was struggling with, he prescribed valium, which helped decrease my anxiety. It also made me sleepy, so I didn't take it regularly. I still had to manage the attacks when they came, but they occurred less often.

With both of us in school, Mark and I didn't have much time with each other. He didn't seem interested in me. Along with that, I worried about not having enough time with Ethan. Vacillating between feeling ignored and feeling guilty, I feared that I was failing as a wife and mother. Because of my troubled history with my own mother, I didn't consider trying to talk with her about my marital life. When I married Mark, she'd handed me a list of things not to do: never serve your husband anything from a can or a jar, never wear curlers at the table, always dress nicely for dinner. While I hadn't always followed her advice, I knew I had to do something to try to get closer to Mark, to try to make our marriage work. Maybe he missed me as well.

The following Friday night I splurged and bought some lamb chops for dinner. It was an ordinary evening, but I wanted to make it special and set the table with elegant linen placemats, a wedding gift, and two twelve-inch candles. Ethan was usually asleep by seven, so we had the evening to ourselves. Mark complimented me on the dinner, but as soon as he finished eating, he went off to his study. Medical school came first, so I was left alone with sputtering candles and dirty dishes.

That night I read in bed for almost two hours, wondering if Mark would show up. When he finally slipped under the covers, I reached for his hand, and he responded with the touch of his fingertips. I turned toward him, but as I began to run my fingers over his shoulder, he tensed up and pulled away.

Did I do something wrong? What's the matter? I asked.

I don't like it when you do that.

I drew back. You mean you don't want me to touch you.

Well, not exactly, it's…it's just that your touch is so light.

I was mystified. He had never complained about my caresses before. Feeling rebuffed, I curled up in a tight ball on my side of the bed and listened to him snore.

We never spoke about that evening. We continued to share the same bed, but we didn't share our dreams or doubts. Our lovemaking was infrequent and unsatisfying, at least for me, and after my failed attempt that night together, I decided that from then on I would let him make the first move. I sensed I didn't please him, but I didn't know what to do about it. It was awkward to talk about sex with him.

But not everything was bad. Although he hardly ever touched me outside of our bedroom, he was an elegant dancer, and sometimes that was how we were able to share some enjoyment and tenderness. Our next-door neighbors often invited us to join them at formal, black-tie dinner dances. As Mark held me in his arms, we spun and glided across the floor like professionals; we knew every step, twist, and dip. It was easy to close my eyes and imagine I was with him in San Francisco before we married, when we were so much in love. We danced fiercely together on those evenings, but the truth was that we seldom connected. We slept with our backs to each other.

Toward the end of my first year in graduate school, I invited one of my classmates, Mary, to live with us. I was trying to make our marriage feel more like a family. Mark was often at the hospital, and I didn't like having dinner alone after putting Ethan to bed. Now, of course, I realize I must have been searching for the friendship, support, and sharing that were missing from my marriage. If Mark was disturbed by her addition to our family, it wasn't obvious.

In May of 1971, when Mary and I graduated, she handed me a slim box wrapped in red gingham cloth. It was a double picture frame: in one frame was a photo of the two of us, arms around each other's waists and big smiles on our faces. In the other frame, she'd written in big, bold blue letters, "Friends multiply our joys and divide our sorrows." Perhaps she knew before I did that Mark and I were headed for trouble.

During that summer, Mark's time away from home increased. His rotation required twenty-four-hour stints at the hospital. As a future doctor's wife, I was supposed to understand, but I felt lonely and abandoned. He had dropped the little niceties, such as expressing how pretty I looked when I wore my hair down. Since we were both gifted at avoiding thorny conversations, we plodded on.

Following graduation, I began work at Planned

Parenthood as director of patient services. It was good to have a full-time job where I felt useful, and my schedule gave me time to pick up Ethan from day care on my way home. I was also immersed in my second year of a three-year postgraduate program, where I was learning how to apply Gestalt principles to psychiatric nursing.

That wasn't all I was learning. The Seventies were a carefree time when many American women, including me, were discovering their sexuality. Curt, a psychologist in my training program, began to show an interest in me in the fall of 1972, during our final year of study. Our affair started in class under the table as he rubbed his foot against my calf. It was exciting to have a man paying attention to me again.

When Curt first held me in his arms, I began to tremble. It had been so long since Mark held me that way that I had almost forgotten I could feel so alive. Starved for affection, and eight years into my marriage, I decided to say yes. Yes, I would meet him for dinner before class; yes, I would meet him at his apartment, where we could make love.

I mentioned to Mark that sometimes I had supper with Curt before classes, hoping for some kind of reaction like, Why aren't you having dinner with your husband? Or, Is there something I don't know about? I looked for anything to indicate he cared, but I couldn't get a rise out of him. We welcomed 1973 at a formal New Year's Eve party but never exchanged a word during the evening. Soon after that, the silence between us exploded. We exchanged cruelties, and I threw one of his bookcases over the banister for emphasis. Later that evening, I told Mark I wanted a divorce.

Mark didn't try to change my mind. He moved out, rented a room, and began his three-year medical residency. As we prepared to sell our home, I made a list of our wedding gifts, separating them into two piles: his family's and mine. When Ethan asked what all the boxes were for, I told him we were taking a big trip but Daddy was staying to work. Maybe I was making a mistake, but I had to find my own way. Our divorce was final in May. Fortunately, the house sold quickly. By early summer I returned to Berkeley, where I had hoped to enter a doctoral program before we left for Ohio. By this time, I recognized that I returned to academia as a remedy when the going got rough.

I used my lover-classmate as a chauffeur to help me drive across the country, but we soon discovered that we didn't have much in common, except broken marriages. Within days he returned to his family, but I had learned I could be a desirable woman.

Once again, I was alone with Ethan, in a house bought almost sight unseen, wondering what to do next. Now I was a single mother and was unprepared for the guilt that haunted me. Each evening Ethan would ask, Mommy, is Daddy coming home for dinner tonight? Each evening I replied he was not. I felt mean-spirited telling my son it would be a long time before he saw his father again. I tried to sound casual, as if living without his father was no big deal, but I sensed an uncertainty in Ethan that hadn't been there before. I began to think that I'd made a colossal mistake. I thought back on our marriage and regretted having cheated on Mark. Yet I realized that I was not a prisoner to anxiety anymore. I went days without giving it a second thought. And I hadn't had a panic attack since I arrived in Berkeley.

One night while Ethan was at camp in the Sierras for two weeks and I had plenty of time alone to think, I called Mark. Can a person who's made a mistake be forgiven? I said, pressing the phone tightly to my ear. I listened to the silence. It was a long time before I heard him say, Sometimes.

We talked late into the night, laying out our gripes and grievances, but this time was different. We listened to each other. Do you think you could come out here for a long weekend? I asked. Can you get away from work? The next day he phoned saying he was flying out to join me for five days. I arranged for Ethan to stay with his godparents, friends of ours since before we were married, while we went up the coast to their oceanside cabin.

It was awkward when Mark met me at my house in his rental car, but after he started to drive north on Highway One, I unwound a little, taking in deep breaths of the salty air. Leaning back, I closed my eyes and drifted into our past as a couple—before Ohio, before Ethan, before we were married. We used to have such fun together, always laughing and teasing each other. Could we be like that again?

It was dusk when we arrived at the cabin. After eating supper, we sat on the porch watching as the sun dropped into the Pacific Ocean. I wanted to put his hand in mine, but I was afraid to touch him. We sat quietly in an accustomed silence. When we finally went inside, the fire we started earlier was scarcely sputtering coals. Well, what do you think? I said, trying to sound nonchalant as I flopped down on the couch.

Mark was quiet. I knew I shouldn't press him. After a long silence he said he thought we ought to renegotiate our marriage agreement.

I wondered what there was to negotiate and asked for some examples.

I don't want you to start the day talking about what's going wrong in the world, he said. Listening to your litany of complaints isn't what I like. I want to get up quietly, undisturbed. He reached for my hand.

I was surprised but didn't let go. Well, I can certainly do that, I said. You might have to remind me until I get the hang of it. What else do you want me to change?

I'm not sure. I'll think about it. I'm tired. Let's go to bed.

Had he decided we'd get back together? It'd been a long time since we'd slept in a double bed. As I moved to the edge, Mark's hand touched my shoulder. I felt a familiar excitement rush through my body. He drew me tightly to him and cradled me in his arms as we made love. It wasn't the passionate love we shared before we married or even in the first years of our marriage; it was reserved: a love that was being tested, a love that didn't have extraordinary expectations.

The sun was up when I awoke the next morning. Mark was on the porch with a cup of coffee. I lay in bed, daydreaming, thinking that our marriage spanned

many of the same years as the Vietnam War. We'd had
our own war, but no one died. Ethan missed his dad,
and I had never really wanted a divorce. I wanted my
husband back: the one I married, the fun-loving seminarian who was both bold and shy. This time I was
determined to make our marriage work, convinced
that our move—so soon after Ethan had been born—
as well as the pressures of medical and graduate school
had been the problem. Perhaps now we could get on
with our lives.

That fall I found a counseling position, Ethan
returned to Montessori school, and Mark was more
than halfway through his first year of residency. In
early November 1973, we held a marriage ceremony
at our home. Ethan was ecstatic as he ran about the
house telling the guests we were having "our wedding."

During the following year, hardly a month went
by without a passionate discussion about where we
should live. I desperately wanted to return to California, but Mark was pleased with his residency in Ohio.
However, he said he was willing to move in the spring
if he could find a medical residency where he could
complete his training. We moved back to Berkeley the
summer of 1974, during the impeachment proceedings
against Nixon. Ethan started first grade in the fall, and
Mark and I took the year off to fall in love with each
other again. We revisited past haunts and investigated
new interests: Mark took up the oboe, over the howling
objections of our corgi, and I found an artisan's studio
where I learned how to weave.

Years later, after I pieced together the timeline of

those years, I figured out that only one year had passed after our remarriage before Mark began his trips to hot johns. No wonder that, in spite of all my efforts, a fog-like, slippery silence existed between us.

Once again, a third adult joined our family. Louis was a graduate student who lived in our guest quarters in exchange for providing some of Ethan's care. We repeated the same pattern as before—adding another adult to our household while we both pursued academic achievement in our professions.

I wanted another child. Mark didn't disagree, but our lovemaking wasn't passionate, merely dutiful. At the time, I didn't know why it took me three years to get pregnant, but later I wondered if it had something to do with his sexual addiction.

The final months of Mark's residency were demanding, and I was lumbering along, seven months pregnant. Fourteen-hour workdays were the norm for him, and he was often snoring loudly before I was ready for bed. One evening as I watched him downing a few swigs of vodka from the quart-sized bottle he kept by the bedside, I said, Why do you drink that stuff at night? I was concerned that his nightly drinks were becoming routine.

It helps me relax, he said in the condescending tone he used when he thought I was interfering with his private space.

There are some good interventions for that kind of problem.

I can take care of myself. He took another slug and turned off his bedside lamp.

Drink all you want, I thought. I have a life to live, one kid to care for, and another on the way. In spite of my irritation, I turned over, patted my stomach, and went to sleep.

Our second child, Alexandra, was born the spring of 1977. She was a healthy, dark-haired, red-faced baby. I was ecstatic to have a little girl—one I could keep this time.

I had just succeeded in establishing a nursing routine with Lexa when Mark announced that he'd been offered a job in a small hospital south of San Francisco, not far from where my parents had a winter home. You want to move next month? I asked in disbelief. Lexa was only a few weeks old, and I was way too tired to think about packing.

I'm serious, he said. If you want to live in the valley, the job that's available wants me there the first of June.

Making the transition from urban to small-town country living turned out to be easier than we had expected. We felt welcomed when Mark was invited to preach at the nearby Episcopal church. Ethan started fourth grade that fall and immediately made friends. I sewed dresses for Lexa, and when she started walking, I returned to my weaving. I put in a vegetable garden: long, silver-green Kentucky wonders; sweet, plump carrots; and luscious cherry tomatoes still warm from the sun. We ate what the garden produced. I made bread from scratch and put up jelly from our quince bush. To everyone, including myself, we looked like a poster family for the happy Seventies. But daily I struggled with anxiety. Whenever I started to do something without Mark nearby, I felt as though I was getting ready for the guillotine. I made a routine for myself, certain places or activities where I felt safe from a panic attack, but I lived in a state of suppressed anxiety every day. I became a very good actress, just as I had been in school.

Within two years, Mark began to chafe in his role as a physician in a small town, so when he was offered the opportunity to teach English part time at Ethan's school, we were both relieved. Not only was he a success as a teacher, but he was appointed to the position of chaplain as well. He was happier than I'd ever seen him. I was glad the man I married had finally returned. He made jokes and told funny stories at dinner again. He asked Ethan to help him with the small greenhouse he was building. He spent time entertaining Lexa. And sometimes I heard him singing.

Ethan and I were engrossed with our 4-H goat projects: birthing, milking, and making cheese and yogurt. Mark, whose hobby was hybridizing flowers, opened a small nursery business with another grower. Our Christmas-card letter that year was filled with all the perfect and enticing events in our lives. I never paused long enough to explore the emptiness and fear that hid our frantic activities.

Then one Saturday morning in March 1982, our lives began to fall apart. The school's head asked Mark to meet with her at ten o'clock. When he returned home an hour later, he looked as if he had been in a battle. Even behind his glasses, his eyes looked bloodshot. His voice was hesitant as he explained that members

of the school board, as well as the diocesan bishop
and the rector of the local Episcopal church, were in
the meeting room when he arrived. He said that his
contract for the next year had been canceled and that
the board had asked for his immediate resignation.
I asked why. He wouldn't look at me. He mumbled
something about the headmistress claiming he wasn't
spending enough time at his job. That made no sense,
since he wasn't home with me during the day.

Alarmed and angry, I said, No one can just cancel
a contract like that. We need to see an attorney. What
would we do if he didn't have a job? He wanted to
walk away. We argued, and finally he agreed to consult
with a lawyer. After a few phone calls back and forth
with the school, the attorney was able to negotiate for
Mark to remain in his position until Ethan graduated
that June.

As president of the parents' organization, I was a
member of the school board, but I had not been asked
to attend that Saturday meeting. Within the week,
Mrs. Waters, one of the board members, invited me to
lunch. She was a longtime friend of my mother's. We
had hardly sat down when she suggested that I resign
from the board. She implied that my recently widowed
mother, whose winter home was in the area, needed to
be spared any news of this "episode," as she called it. I
felt as though I was being blackmailed. It was a small
community. I knew we'd have to leave.

Three months later, we moved south of San Francisco. Ethan left for boarding school on the East Coast.
My nest was half-empty, and I missed his energy and

wit. I needed him to soften the hard silence that was building between Mark and me.

Mark spent a lot of time alone in his den, struggling with a word processor. He couldn't find a teaching position but was able to collaborate with another physician in writing a book about medical care. In between chapters, Mark managed the financial aspects of the flower business, mostly by phone. One day on my way out of the drugstore, I saw a magazine with the word "panic" printed in large letters across its cover. I quickly read the article and discovered that a psychiatrist had a name for the terror I had lived with for so long. So I wasn't the only one who had that struggle! When I returned home, I ran upstairs to tell Mark that I had a label—"anxiety disorder"—and that with some serious work, I could get my panic under control. Mark looked up from his computer, frowning as I explained that I would be learning how not to be so dependent on him.

He sat calmly in his chair and returned to his typing. Why wasn't he ecstatic about what I had learned?

Years later I realized how my independence would have been a threat to him. Only then did I begin to understand that my anxiety had prevented me from seeing how Mark used our marriage and his professions, physician and priest, as camouflage.

It was 1984 when I finally succeeded in convincing Mark to move us near my hometown, Madison, Wisconsin. I argued that since his part of the plant business was done by phone, he shouldn't have any trouble relocating. No doubt tired of my nagging by then, Mark finally agreed to go.

We bought land on the outskirts of Madison, moved to a nearby rental home, hired a contractor, and acted as our own architects. Ground was broken in September. Two young Nubian goats, vestiges of our 4-H project, arrived in April. We happily celebrated Easter 1985 in our new house.

Looking back, building a home was a diversionary tactic for both of us. It kept us busy and gave us something to talk about instead of focusing on our own challenges and our shaky marriage. We did that in our first marriage, so by now we were both skilled at avoidance and denial. Furthermore, we put the mysterious humiliation of Mark's firing behind us. I don't recall that we ever mentioned it again.

Our marriage and family life seemed to be moving along without any extraordinary road bumps. In 1986, Ethan took a year off between high school and college to do volunteer work and design computer programs. Lexa, now in eighth grade, was waiting for the first snow so she could go skiing. Mark was often busy talking on the phone with his business partner in California, trying to determine what plants would sell best in the marketplace. He was pleased when he was asked to serve on the local bishop's advisory commission on AIDS. It gave him the opportunity to wear both of his professional hats: physician and priest. We had adjusted to a certain distance but were congenial for the most part. By then, we'd been together over twenty years, and we knew and tolerated one another's quirks.

As it turned out, it was fortunate that we moved when we did. I was about to get the biggest shock of my life. If I hadn't been in my hometown, where I had many compassionate and caring friends and my family's support system, I don't know how I would have survived.

Decade of Denial

> People want to get better, but they don't want to change.
>
> —*A Wise Psychiatrist*

Two weeks had passed since Mark had admitted to being a sexual addict, and I was still numb from the shock of his revelation. We'd had three meetings with two addiction counselors and had officially entered treatment with them. Despite my background in nursing and psychology, I had no idea what to expect. I just wanted my husband to stop being a sex addict.

Both of us were assigned a counselor to act as a support person: a man, Dr. Anthony Taylor, for Mark, and a woman, Dr. Susan Blume, for me.

What is your sexual history? This was the first question Dr. Blume asked me.

What does my sexual behavior have to do with Mark's addiction? I answered. He's the sex addict, not me. All I had was a few months' fling with a man while I was married. At the time, I guess, I felt I deserved it. Mark didn't seem interested in me. But I knew it wasn't right. I never betrayed him after we remarried in 1974.

I was ticked off about having to talk to Dr. Blume. I didn't think my intimate life was any of her business. I'd never had to talk to anyone before about it. I didn't see what it had to do with Mark's problems. But these counselors were supposed to be the best in the city. So I told her about the baby I had when I was nineteen. I told Mark before we were engaged, I said. I wanted him to know that he was marrying a woman who, back then, was considered used goods. He didn't seem at all concerned. I had shared my secret with him. I wish he'd told me his.

During one of our earliest sessions, we were instructed not to have sex for at least six months. That was fine by me; we didn't have much sex anyway. We were advised to find other ways of being intimate. Looking back now, I realize that we made some mistakes. We weren't a couple who enjoyed many ways of being close, and at the time, that was the last thing I wanted to be with Mark. Back then, neither our counselors nor I recognized that I needed more time to work through my grief as well as the chance to reestablish my physical and emotional sense of safety. Furthermore, our counselors never brought up the fact that Mark was only having sex with men. I didn't either. Not in front of the counselors, that is. I had asked him myself, why only men, why not women? He said that sex with women was always more complicated—more demands were made. He was right. Women do expect more than just a quickie in a public john, and I never questioned him further than that. My mistake.

We were both directed to attend twelve-step groups. Mark went to SAA (Sexual Addicts Anonymous) on Sunday evenings, and I attended COSA (Codependents of Sexual Addicts) on Tuesday nights in the basement of a nearby church. Before I was allowed to join the group, I had to be interviewed by a COSA member and provide a letter of introduction from my counselor. COSA was in its infancy at the time, understandably below the radar, and meetings weren't publicized as they are now.

We met at a Burger King for coffee. The COSA group representative was polite but edgy, frequently glancing over her shoulder as she spoke to me. She stated that everything said in the meetings was confidential and added that no phone numbers were exchanged. Having to give her a rundown on my situation was torturous. I hadn't shared that information with anyone except the counselors. I felt exposed and humiliated. When I arrived at the church the following night for my first meeting, my stomach was churning. I couldn't imagine that anyone felt as degraded as I did. I thought I would be criticized. I was completely surprised when I was warmly welcomed instead.

The world that the women described at each meeting was alien to me. Their accounts were filled with lovers and husbands who abused drugs and alcohol, used porn, and were often physically abusive. Some mentioned that pornography was a big part of their partners' lives. I listened in astonished silence to their stories of anger and despair. Not one group member practiced safe sex, yet all knew their spouses had sex with other women. It seemed to me that an ugly game of Russian roulette—with lives at stake—was being played out behind ordinary suburban doors.

I never told anyone else what was happening between Mark and me, not for thirteen years, not my brother and not my closest friends. I was too ashamed.

On one of those Sunday nights when Mark was at his meeting and Lexa was on an overnight at a friend's house, I felt unusually apprehensive. I paced anxiously from room to room. Who was I? The man in my bed at night had been living a life of fornication and promiscuity. He was my husband; what did that make me? Unclean? My body tensed as I heard Mark's car drive into the garage.

Hi, I'm home, he shouted as he opened the back door and walked into the kitchen.

Mark, this may sound strange, but I need to scrub you clean.

He came to an abrupt halt and looked intently at me. All right. What should I do?

I told him to go to our shower and motioned to him to undress. Get in, I said turning on the hot water. Without a word, he stepped inside the stall and faced the faucet. I began to wash him. I scoured him up and down with the bath brush, thinking perhaps I could rid his body of all the dreadfulness it carried. I want to cleanse you.

I know, he said, turning around to face me as he

stepped out of the shower. He reached for a towel. His skin blazed a fiery red. I knew what had happened couldn't be undone.

By the time Ethan came home for the Christmas holidays, Mark and I had been in counseling for more than a month. Mark didn't want to tell him about his addiction, but the counselors emphasized what we already knew: secrets are filled with shame and guilt and become more toxic the longer they are kept hidden. It was clear that cover-ups had already damaged our marriage. We were certain that Ethan and Lexa were experiencing confusion and disconnects. Occasionally we quarreled in front of them, something we rarely did before Mark's admission. Believing that Lexa, age ten, was too young to understand, we only brought Ethan with us to our next session.

As Mark began explaining his trips to men's rooms during the last dozen years, Ethan's eyes filled with tears. I knew why I didn't have a dad when I was little, he said. You were always away at med school. Now I know why I didn't have one when I was growing up either. Ethan looked older than his twenty years. His face was etched with pain. He walked slowly across the room and put his hand on Mark's shoulder. I'm sorry for you, Dad.

I wanted to shout out loud: Look what you've done to our son. But I swallowed my words and quenched my sorrow in the pit of my stomach.

Mark didn't apologize. Instead, he slumped in his chair, twisting his wedding ring. We all sat motionless.

Dr. Taylor finally said, I guess that's all for today. All of you have a lot to discuss when you get home.

I followed Mark as he quickly left the room. Now I wasn't alone with Mark and his secret—Ethan had joined us. As painful as that was for him, at least we wouldn't have to pretend all the time. I thought having Mark's secret out in the open would help Mark and me deal with the realities of our family, but it only amplified the barriers between us.

It was dusk when drove away from the clinic. The snow was falling quickly, wrapping us in silence. The oncoming headlights poked through the evening sleet, reminding me of a funeral procession.

Ethan went directly to his room and didn't come to dinner. Mark and I restricted our conversation to monosyllables. Leaving the dishes for Mark, I excused myself and went downstairs. For a second I stopped in front of Ethan's door, and then hesitantly knocked on it. Ethan, it's me. May I come in?

Sure thing, he answered. He was lying on his bed, his eyes bloodshot and puffy from crying.

I can't fix it, Ethan, but I can hold you. I took him in my arms, and we held each other. I'm so very sorry. We'll get through this, though. I promise you.

Yah, I know. He held my hand. The next morning Ethan left for college. I thought a door had closed between him and his father. I hoped I wouldn't lose him too.

With Ethan gone, I felt again a vast emptiness. What had happened to the man I met so many years before in San Francisco—the one who laughed, wrote poetry, and sang, the one who teased and loved me? I didn't know it at the time, but deep within I began to grieve the mate I'd already lost. Why had he betrayed us? Was it my anxiety disorder that made him deceive me? Surely he could have told me, issued an ultimatum, given me a warning.

I spilled my confusion and bottled-up fury onto the pages of my journal and continued to see Frances, the counselor who had urged me to reconcile with my mother before she died. I was gaining more control over my anxiety, so sometimes I drove myself to her office instead of asking Mark to take me. That was a breakthrough. I was a little less dependent on him, but clearly, it was not enough.

I was in the grip of a massive anxiety disorder, but none of the physicians or psychiatrists whom I consulted during that time in the late Eighties and early Nineties indicated how debilitated I really was. Or perhaps they did and I didn't hear them because my denial was so immense. I couldn't hop in the car to meet a friend for lunch, not unless I knew Mark would be nearby. I had a cell phone for the car. It helped me feel more secure, knowing I could call him at any time. But I was not the free spirit I wanted to be. I was on medication. It took the edge off, but I wasn't "cured."

Each morning after Lexa left for school, I cleaned up the kitchen and readied myself for the day, but I made no headway. I had little energy and no direction. I was trying to understand what had happened to us. I still thought I could fix it, fix him, and fix us.

Thinking back to the early years of our marriage, when we lived in Ohio, I realized that I had begun to sense Mark's distancing even then. Like an irritated amoeba, he withdrew if I even lightly brushed his shoulder. I thought in some ways he'd been angry all his life: angry because he grew up with an alcoholic mother, angry because his father was absent during the war, angry because his parents divorced, and angry because his father left him with his mother. Mark once explained that as a young boy he dealt with his emotional pain— he carefully avoided the word anger—by withdrawing to his room and reading books. Perhaps now he stuffed his feelings inside, but instead of taking refuge in his books, he visited men's johns, hoping he could find sexual release and intimacy among strangers. Buried deep in my own sorrow, I overlooked the fact that emotional pain often suffocates a cry for help.

I remember one terrible scene. It was fall 1972. We were in Elmwood Heights. Mark was in his last year of medical school, and I was working as a nurse at Planned Parenthood. We were both seeing our respective therapists. Aaron, my counselor, had suggested we might have a session with Mark and his counselor, Ben, to work on improving our communication skills. Mark and I agreed, and the following week we met in Ben's office.

They both stood up when Aaron and I walked in. Mark moved quickly to the yellow beanbag chair and stretched out his legs on the floor. When we got home, I slammed the car door and went immediately into my study. I wrote the following in my journal:

We were talking about misunderstandings. Mark announced that I never seemed to be satisfied with what he gave me. Without any warning he stripped off his clothes, crossed his legs, and covering his privates, he looked straight at me. Here I am, take all of me, he said. I was appalled. Aaron and Ben said nothing. Immediately I felt that Mark's action was hostile, his words sarcastic. At a deeper level his actions set up a game of three against one, three men against one woman, a collusion against me, a declaration that implied: what's the matter with you for not wanting my body? But there was something peculiar about Mark's exposure. Was he displaying himself to Aaron and Ben? His exhibitionism wasn't inclusive of me. It was an angry, invasive rejection of me. For a second, I sensed a homosexual aspect to his display. He was showing himself to them, not to me.

At the time, I closed my journal and put it back under my mattress. I didn't know it then, but within seconds, the impenetrable wall of denial enveloped me. When I looked at my journal the next day, I turned the page. I didn't look back on that journal until years later.

Subsequently, in November 1987, the morning I woke up and asked Mark if he was homosexual, my intuition *was* right. However, I didn't trust it. I was scared of what I didn't want to know.

Some years later, I mentioned the incident to a psychiatrist friend of mine. She said that Mark's behavior was absolutely nuts. I laughed, saying her choice of words was not exactly clinical. Clinical sometimes isn't adequate was her quick response.

Several times during our marriage, I sought help from psychiatrists for my anxiety attacks. One gave me the book he was writing and asked me to give him feedback. Another was so overweight that I knew immediately he had more to deal with than I did. Then in early 1990, I found a psychiatrist who not only believed in learning to live with anxiety in a healthier way but also suggested that I try one of the drugs recommended to soften awful frights like mine. My anxiety didn't go away, but it no longer dominated my daily life. I was able to venture a little farther from home in the car. Sometimes I even shopped for groceries by myself. I wasn't cured, but I was feeling more self-sufficient.

Mark continued to attend his weekly SAA meetings. I quit attending within half a year. Several women in the group suggested putting a detective on my husband, as they had theirs, but that didn't seem right to me. I wasn't ready to hear how long they had struggled with their husbands without any of the men changing their behavior.

In spite of all the things I was doing, constantly worrying about my marriage had emotionally imprisoned and isolated me. I missed Edith and wished she were nearby to hold me in her arms. But I couldn't tell her what had happened to us. She had made the bread for the communion service at our wedding. It would break her heart to know about our struggle now.

I remembered one time when Edith was making

cookies with Ethan. Lexa was still in her walker—zooming across the linoleum floor, smearing yogurt all over her face. Ethan was grinning as he swung the cookie sheet back and forth through the air. I'm making it cool faster, Mom, so that we can make more cookies.

Edith was laughing, her blue eyes twinkling, her wavy white hair glowing around her face. We're not making cookies, you know, she said. We're making memories.

How I wished I could go back to that time. Maybe there was something I could have done differently. Perhaps Mark and I could have been kinder to one another.

We stumbled through the next two years. We were approaching our twenty-fifth wedding anniversary, if we didn't count the six-month divorce in 1973. I think we were both terrified of being honest with ourselves. At the time, being gay was a societal shame, and I was scared that I couldn't manage my life without him because of my anxiety attacks. I was totally dependent on Mark and didn't want to admit it.

He regularly attended his twelve-step program, and I thought we were making our way through the jungle. In a self-congratulatory moment when things between us seemed peaceful, we decided to take a chance. We celebrated our twenty-fifth anniversary and renewed our marriage vows.

Our diocesan bishop performed the service in mid-May in our living room. Several family members and friends who'd been at our wedding in 1965 were present. Of course, Edith was there. I hoped that after such bitterness and anger, Mark and I at last had come to a place of forgiveness and understanding. If only I had been bold and totally candid with myself.

But I wasn't. I accepted the renewal as an outward expression of our victory over betrayal, when actually it was more like learning to live with what I didn't like. In a corner of my mind, one fact still gnawed at me: Lexa had never been told that her father was wrestling with an addiction. It wasn't anything we talked about anymore. Now I thought she had a right to know. Mark did not. He'd rather die than tell Lexa where he stood.

The following evening, we hosted a party with dinner and dancing at a nearby country club. Lexa, now thirteen, wore a pink-and-white floral dress. Ethan brought a date with him from college, a lovely young woman named Angela, who—as I expected—became his wife a few years later.

After the celebration, much like many newlyweds, we made a little world for ourselves. We bought an abandoned twelve-acre hobby farm a twenty-minute drive from our home. The greenhouses Mark and his business partner owned in California had flourished, and they thought the timing was right to introduce colorful tropical plants to dreary Midwestern winters. The old brick farmhouse made a perfect office. There was space to add a laboratory when the business could afford it. It took more than year to build the greenhouse where the pastures had once been. When it was finished, ten thousand square feet housed the growing areas, office, boilers, huge water tanks, and potting area. I was relieved to have a focus that was not Mark's addiction. But deep within I recognized we were living an armed truce, and what we were keeping from our daughter made me sad and apprehensive.

The first shipment of young plants from the California branch arrived in early spring 1992. Lexa, now sixteen, and some of her friends helped pot them up. The workspace rocked with music of U2 and Arrested Development as the kids jockeyed to see who was the fastest potter. It was a bright and happy place to work. The staff was talented and conscientious, and the flowers were impressive in color and form. We made a little community for our employees and ourselves. In time, it became a place where I think we all felt safe with one another. What I recognized later was that it gave me space to reflect and to grow. As I cultivated the flowers in my care, I replenished my own soul.

It didn't take me long to learn the care and feeding of various plants, and when the business added a botanist and a lab, I became a hybridizer. I was curious to see what happened when one species crossed with another. I harvested seeds smaller than grains of sand and took them in envelopes to the laboratory. Eighteen months later, many of them arrived back in the greenhouse as seedlings, ready to be potted. The first time they bloomed, I could recognize their unique features: bright yellows with dark spots in the center that looked like tears, and deep reds with black markings that looked like little faces. I was absorbed in their care. I wasn't paying attention to my own feelings and concerns.

In those early years of the business, Mark's mood

seemed good, but he could turn sour in a split second, so I never knew what to expect. Nonetheless, it was easy to lose myself in the daily routine of caring for the flowers: watering, fertilizing, and checking air movement, temperature, and light—all according to schedule. Sometimes Mark and I worked side by side, enjoying the plants, the heady scents, the tropical warmth, and the grow lights. We both pretended that the business was a success, even when the monthly statements revealed that it was in the red. Beneath all the pretending, we were still emotionally distant. Without noticing it, we both entered into an illusion. I was glad he didn't want to abandon me and thankful that what had threatened our marriage had a name—despite its being labeled "sexual addiction"—and Mark seemed to be relieved to have the secret off his chest. I did my best to believe that addictions could be managed.

It was a fragile time for me. I lost many of the older people who had been close to me. I felt left behind, asked too soon to be the eldest in my family. My mother died in 1992. After that, all the Norwegian uncles and aunties in my dear Edith's family died, and too soon, Edith herself left us. She went to sleep one night and didn't wake up the next morning. Why did Edith have to leave me? I had depended on her my entire life. I always knew she was there, a protection against the monsters under the bed and the chilling thoughts that nothing lay ahead.

Mark gave Edith's eulogy. I sat rigidly in the pew in front of him. How could he comfort the congregation with his words when at home he turned away from

me? Now both my mothers were dead, and I felt alone
and vulnerable. The dimensions of my life changed: I
no longer had a generation between death and me.

All too soon, Lexa graduated and went off to
college. It was 1995. I didn't realize how much she was
a part of me until she left. My arms ached to hold her,
and I held silent conversations with her as I lay awake
at night. For thirty years, I had had at least one child
at home, and now there were none. The house sounded
unusually quiet without her voice ringing out, without
her stories about friends, without her opinions. I missed
holding her hand when we sat together on the couch.

Within weeks of Lexa leaving, one of my closest
friends, Ruthie, died. She had inoperable cancer and
used to spend a few hours weekly at the nursery. She
would open the greenhouse door, a radiant smile on
her face, and slowly make her way toward the potting
area. As she would pass the office bench, she'd wink
at the staff and twist her wig around. How does my
hair look today, she'd ask. She never failed to get a
chuckle out of one of us. Mark would guide Ruthie to
her favorite chair—the one with a bright red pillow—
and help her get seated. Sitting down next to her, he
would ask with a twang to his voice, Wanna work hard
today or just take a break?

How did I do last time? she always asked.

Just fine, he would answer.

Well then, let's do it again. And they dug in. He
handed her a plant, its roots already dusted with repot-
ting formula, and together they potted, very slowly, for
an hour or two. Ruthie enjoyed having people around

her. She was an inspiring testimony of grace and courage. I wanted to share with her what had happened between Mark and me. I thought she'd understand. But I was never brave enough to risk it, and after she became sick, I didn't want to tell her. Next to what she faced, I figured my problem was simply a bend in the road.

Mark and I managed to masquerade our way through the years leading to the twenty-first century, but when he and his business partner decided to part company, Mark's branch of the business took a hit. The older California business was in good financial shape, but Mark's setup was having money problems. If he couldn't get bargain-priced shipments of plants from his former partner, it was going to be even harder for his business to turn a profit. Mark grew more depressed and surly than before the downturn. I helped his business as much as possible. I had inherited some money at my parents' death. Although I enjoyed my job, it was not my ambition, and I was growing crotchety around the edges. Then the bottom fell out.

Mark purchased stock, ready to bloom, and my crop of young flowers was tossed to make room for sale-ready plants. Tray by tray I pitched them into black trash bags—growing more furious with each one I dumped. I had looked forward each day to seeing which seedlings had bloomed overnight in what I called my pediatric ward. The flowers were a gift of life and success, and I wasn't having much of that in my own personal life. As I heaved bags full of flowers onto the

dump cart, I felt I was discarding parts of myself. At a
deeper level, I think I recognized that the business was
going to fail and so were Mark and I.

It shouldn't have been a surprise when my body
said, *Enough stress*. Shortly after midnight, in the
spring of 1998, I awakened with my pulse racing faster
than Mark could count. Call 911, I yelled. The para-
medics arrived, hooked me up to an IV, and drove me
off to the hospital. I had several tests and was given
medication to slow my heart rate. After my vital signs
had stabilized, Mark drove us home, but before I was
able to see my own doctor, the same thing happened
again the next night. Call 911 for the medics, I said, my
pulse racing like before.

You don't need an ambulance, he said, holding the
phone out of my reach. I'll take you in the car.

I was afraid I was going to die. But you can't take
care of me, I yelled at him.

I won't go with you, then.

Grabbing the phone from him, I dialed 911. Then
I called my friend Kris, who lived close by. Quickly, I
told her what had happened and asked if she would
ride in the ambulance with me. She said she'd be right
over.

This time I was admitted into the hospital and
released the next day with an appointment already
arranged with my internist. He reviewed my records
from the ER, and, after ruling out all the usual physical
causes, he said I probably knew as well as he did what
the problem was.

Stress? I said.

He nodded. When are you going to do something about that?

I told him I was seeing a counselor, and he replied that that might not be enough. I thought at the time that he was signaling that there seemed to be a lot of tension in my marriage. He was Mark's doctor, too, and might have been privy to information I didn't have.

I called Ethan that night, just to hear his reassuring voice. I told him what had happened and how his dad had been so angry with me for calling the ambulance. Giving his usual casual chuckle, he said, Mom, he's angry. You took his job away from him.

What do you mean?

I mean you can really take care of yourself. You don't need *him* to do that. His voice was firm and reassuring.

Okay, I guess I'll think about that, I said. Maybe there really wasn't any point in my trying to save our marriage. Maybe we should separate for a time, just to get some perspective.

First the doctor and now my son were trying to send me signals. I saw the signs, but like whispers in the night, they were forgotten or dismissed in the morning. I needed some time to sort myself out. What I really needed was courage.

6

Masks

The most important kind of freedom is to be who you really are. You trade in your reality for a role. You give up your ability to feel, and in exchange, put on a mask. You give up your sense for an act.

—*Jim Morrison*

As the months went by, Mark walked guardedly, as though in pain. I knew his back bothered him, and he seemed discouraged. He switched psychiatrists and found a doctor who prescribed a new combination of medications for him, but his moods were dark, and he didn't sleep well at night. His breathing was jagged and uneven. Sometimes he gasped for air. I was certain he had sleep apnea. I asked him to see our doctor. He refused. I wanted him to sleep in another room, but as a nurse, I knew if he had sleep apnea, he might die in the middle of the night.

We continued to have our verbal go-rounds. I

wanted things clarified. Mark didn't want to talk. He was good at the silent treatment. We were caught in a vicious cycle, and neither of us was able to escape.

Spring of 2000 arrived, and I hoped that spending time at our usual vacation spot, a dude ranch in Arizona, would provide a different perspective on our predicament. Shortly before our departure, I received an article from a physician whose research on porn and cybersex addiction was due to be published in the coming months. The forty-page study analyzed married men's involvement with porn and cybersex and the effect it had on their marriages. The article concluded that wives experienced the virtual act to be as devastating as if it had been real. I could certainly identify with that.

I gave the article to Mark and told him it was important to me that he read the material before we left home. For several months now, he had been insisting that his time on the Internet was his business. My view was: not when his actions betrayed our marriage. Mark remained rigidly clear about his opinion. I remained just as clear on the other side of the fence.

As we sat down to dinner that night, he said in a flat voice, I've been thinking that the poison you feel in our relationship is the anger I'm feeling all the time.

I was astonished. He never admitted to being angry. If I ever tried to suggest he might be mad he'd reply, I'm not angry. You're the one who's angry.

He was right about that. I had often been at the edge of fury since I first knew of his betrayal. But this time I sensed he was saying something different to me.

I don't know what it is, Mark, but there is something basically wrong between us, I said. It has something to do with anger, and my gut tells me that you know something I don't. I didn't add that I thought it had something to do with the *why* of his being angry. We talked a little more, pushing my statement around like the edge of an envelope.

What you've done in the past has caused me a lot of pain, I said. You still do because you're emotionally unavailable. I don't know how to be with you anymore. I folded my napkin and put it next to my plate as I waited for his reply. He remained silent, so I continued. You've never apologized to me, so I've concluded you don't want to. In other words, neither our marriage nor our children are top priorities in your life.

I'm so tired of hearing you complain, he said. We've been over this so many times. I'm tired of listening to what you don't like about me.

Well, what do you expect? Our marriage has been violently damaged. It's like a death has occurred and we're standing around waiting for the funeral to begin.

Mark didn't know that I had made an appointment to see a lawyer when we returned. I was getting ready to end our marriage.

I don't know what to say, Mark muttered. It's hard for me to be any different.

Hard for you to stop committing adultery? Mark, do you know what you're saying?

Just stop, he pleaded. Stop talking. I can't stand it when you go on and on like this.

We sat in silence. Minutes passed. This is ridiculous,

I thought. I picked up our dinner plates and headed to the kitchen.

My hands shook as I set the dishes next to the sink. Raising my voice, I said, I'm going to stop talking to you altogether. When you want me to be in a conversation with you, you'll have to say so.

Don't do that! said Mark.

I *will* do that. I feel like a guest in my own home. You don't want to listen to me, and you don't want to speak to me. There's nothing else I can do.

I was starting to open the refrigerator door when Mark trudged into the room and stood across the center island from me. The room was bright and silent like a hospital OR waiting for the morning's first patient.

Please turn around with your back to me, he said in a firm voice. I don't want you to face me.

Slowly I turned my back to him. I tried to swallow. Was he going to knife me in the back? The drawers with knives were on my side of the center island, but I couldn't remember if I'd left any out when I made dinner.

I read that article about cybersex you gave me, he said. It's like a record of the Holocaust. He paused for a moment. I feel I'm the Nazi.

Be careful, I thought to myself. Will he explode or not? Very softly, I said, You are.

The air was still. I grasped my hands together in front of me, and very slowly, I twisted my watch around my wrist so that I could see its face. Glancing down, I saw that seven minutes had passed and asked, May I turn around now?

No, not yet, he said. I don't want you to see me right now.

Okay. I'll stay here just as I am. I tried to sound reassuring, uncertain what he might do. My heart pounded in my ears. Ten more minutes passed in silence. May I turn around now? I whispered.

Yes, said Mark. He was sitting on the kitchen stool; his head lowered; his hands open on the tiled surface in front of him.

You don't have to read that material again, I offered.

Yes, I do. I need to read it every day. I see your face everywhere in it.

I am everywhere in it, I replied.

I waited for him to leave the kitchen, relieved that there weren't any knives on the kitchen counters. I was exhausted. No doubt, Mark would stay up late bending over the computer in his downstairs den. I was going to bed.

Two days later we left for our annual trip to the Southwest. As he drove, I tried again to reach out to him—reminiscing about other springtimes and our hopes for the future of his business. His comments were limited to either I don't know or Can't we talk about that later?

It was the first time in many years that we'd made the long car trip without Lexa. I was worried about being alone with Mark and so far from home base. But I was relieved that as the miles passed, he seemed to mellow out a little. We kept our conversation to the scenery and the particular horses we hoped to ride.

Three days later, we pulled into snowy Flagstaff

and spent the night at seven thousand feet. It was clear and cold the next morning as Mark guided the car onto the slippery freeway and headed south. Suddenly, the car veered off the road, missing a Ponderosa pine by inches. What's wrong? I yelled. I grabbed for the door handle and braced myself as the car skidded to one side.

I don't know, he said. I think I fell asleep. You better drive.

Of course. Do you know what happened? I adjusted the mirrors and steered the car back onto the highway.

I felt fine this morning; I drank two cups of coffee. Now I feel sort of tired. His face was chalk white.

I assured him I could drive, and within a mile, Mark was asleep. We were lucky the snow was heavy with moisture, or we might have plunged into the narrow canyon below. Slowly, so as not to wake him, I took his pulse. It was steady, regular, as was his breathing. I wondered if he had suffered a small stroke.

The next morning, Mark admitted that he had a headache and hadn't slept well. Begrudgingly he agreed to consult a neurologist before leaving Tucson for the ranch. The diagnosis was what I'd suspected—sleep apnea. He was told not to drive until he had an overnight hospital evaluation. Our vacation was a disappointment. Mark was sullen most of the time, and I was worried about what the sleep apnea testing might lead to.

Two weeks later, after we returned home to Madison, Mark stayed in the hospital, hooked up to the machines, and the diagnosis was confirmed. The doctor told Mark there was no way of knowing if he'd suffered any loss of mental function over the years. I stole a look at Mark and touched his hand. He grimaced as if he were in physical pain. I ached for him—I knew what kind of a blow he'd just taken. He wouldn't be able to bear the thought that his competence might in any way be compromised. His quick mind and sharp wit were talents that he valued, and they were qualities I admired in him.

Mark's treatment included nightly air delivered by a CPAP machine, which forced air into his lungs. The respiratory therapist had told him to sleep in a room by himself until he got comfortable with the mask, but Mark insisted on sleeping in our bed.

That evening he wrestled with the machine while he meticulously explained to me the adjustments he was making. Damn it, I'm going to make this thing work, he said, twisting the stiff plastic hose onto the flow generator. I didn't want to irritate him by asking questions, so I watched quietly as he struggled with the equipment. Finally, he got the mask fixed the way he wanted and slumped back onto his pillows. I was struck by the irony of that mask. I had begun to realize that he'd been masked throughout our marriage.

The machine made a rhythmic swishing sound. Can you hear me? I pointed to my ears and lips. I saw his mask move and then heard something that sounded like a dishwasher warming up.

I shook my head and mouthed, I can't understand you. What if he needed me in the middle of the night? What if I needed him? He lay in bed, eyes closed, trying to learn the rhythm of the machine. His legs shuffled around on the bed in a slow dance. I watched him for almost a half-hour before he fell asleep.

The CPAP machine sat on the floor next to Mark's side of the bed, chugging and woofing, while I sat wide awake with my bedside light on, trying to read myself to sleep. I got up and made myself some warm milk. When that didn't work, I put wax earplugs in my ears and covered my head with pillows. I lay staring into the darkness until long after midnight. All of a sudden, I felt a stream of cold, wet air blowing on the back of my neck. I heard a crash and then gurgling. I flicked on my night light. Mark was sitting up in bed, unmasked, staring at the CPAP hose. It had become unplugged from the machine and was whirling around above our headboard.

How odd we must have looked—my wet hair, his broken machine. There we sat, tired and confused by the unexpected turn our lives had taken. The next evening, I found Mark sitting on the edge of our bed, weeping as he held his mask. I took his hand and held it against my cheek. I'm sorry, I said. I wish there was something I could do.

It was clear that he wouldn't be sleeping in our bed anytime soon. I had wanted to ask him to leave a while ago, but I hadn't found the words to say good-bye.

Sleep apnea accentuated the distance that already existed between us. Mark focused on the consequences of his sleep apnea while I brooded over our marriage. That next night, before he went down to Ethan's room to sleep, he said, We might as well hug each other. No one else is going to. He reached out and took me in his arms. I remembered how gently he had held me in the past. I didn't know it then, but it would be the last time we shared our marriage bed.

As the weeks went by, Mark seemed to adjust to his sleep machine; nonetheless, he was frequently irritable during the day and would wander off to a corner of the greenhouse to sleep. I felt threatened yet relieved by the distance his sleep apnea created between us. Whether we meant to or not, we were building an impenetrable wall between us. But I still didn't have the guts to call it quits, to walk out on my husband, who was obviously ill.

We decided to spend the Fourth of July weekend at our lake cabin north of Madison. I awoke to clear skies and only a few whitecaps dotting the deep blue water of Lake Superior. It was a perfect day for hiking the forest trails or searching for rocks along the beach. I asked Mark if he wanted to join me. He muttered something about needing to work on the business's webpage. During the last few years, his laptop had become his constant companion—another convenient wedge between us. I'll go alone then, I said, and stomped out the door.

The lake swells broke close to the beach as I searched for agates along the shoreline. After walking almost a mile, I reached my favorite rocky point. The sun had warmed the boulders, and I lay down to soak up their heat as I watched the seagulls lazily crisscross the sky. I must have fallen asleep. When I opened my eyes, clouds were forming, and the air had grown cool.

It was late afternoon when I finally entered the cabin. The fading sunlight fell on the oak floor. Hearing the *click-click* of computer keys in the den, I pushed open the door. Spinning around in his chair, Mark slammed down his computer screen, but not before I caught a glimpse of naked bodies. Porn? Cybersex? I yanked off my wedding ring and threw it at him. It rolled under his chair. What the hell do you think you're doing? I'm on to you this time. How long have you been up to this stuff?

It's none of your business. He picked up my ring and stuck it in his shirt pocket.

Not my business? It certainly is *my* business, and it's *our* marriage business.

What I do on the net is none of your concern, he replied.

Yes it is. You're my husband. And you've had a relapse. You should have stayed in your twelve-step program.

You told me you didn't want me to be away in the evenings, so I quit. It seems I'm never able to please you.

Stop trying to blame me for what you do. You'd better pack tonight, I said. We're leaving tomorrow, early, and I'm driving. I slammed the door behind me. I wasn't going to take another chance with his driving.

The following morning, as I settled into the driver's seat and pulled onto the scenic highway, I said, You do talk to your therapist about relapses don't you? I wanted to punch him in the nose, but that wasn't going to get me anywhere.

I've only been seeing her for a year. We're concentrating on my depression. He took off his glasses and wiped them on his shirttail.

Have you told her you're a sex addict? I tried to sound indifferent, but he knew me better than that. I couldn't pull it off. He knew I was furious.

He spoke in a flat voice. No. I haven't decided if I trust her yet.

That doesn't make any sense, Mark. You take the meds she prescribes for you. I glanced over at him. He was carefully studying the passing scenery. Tell me you weren't looking at pornography. I gripped the steering wheel.

No, I won't tell you that, because I was.

How long have you been doing that? I remembered what the women in my COSA group had said about porn, and I didn't know if I wanted to hear his answer.

I told you yesterday. I don't want to talk about it.

Within minutes, his rasping snores filled the car. His sleep apnea provided him a total escape from me. Years ago the women in my COSA group had talked about the inevitability of porn and cybersex. I was so terribly scared at the time that I didn't want to hear. I didn't think my husband could fall that low.

A month later, as we were finishing dinner, Mark mentioned something about his addiction. He'd seen his therapist earlier in the day, so I was immediately on guard. Concentrating on his dinner plate, he began to talk. I need to tell you some things about my problem. He stopped and took a deep breath and then began to speak. From the time when I first acted out, in '75, until twelve years later, when I first told you about it back in '87...

I put my hands over my ears. My God, he'd been notified that someone he'd been with had AIDS.

Gale, listen to me. He raised his voice. During that time, I had about twelve hundred contacts.

My stomach lurched. I did the math. Twelve hundred contacts in twelve years, one hundred a year— that meant he had two contacts a week. I stared at him in disbelief. *Twelve hundred?* I said.

Yes. And then there were about four more times this last year. His face was pale.

Slowly, I rose up from my chair, and without looking at him again, I left the room. Trying to hold myself together, I tore down the hallway to my bedroom and collapsed on the bed. The man who had promised to love and cherish me had continually betrayed me. Twelve hundred times. I buried my head in the pillows. I wanted to die. Exhausted from crying, I finally fell asleep.

The next morning, Mark walked into our bedroom as if nothing had happened. I was brushing my teeth, and I didn't want to be near him. I turned away, my body language demanding privacy.

In my mind, I began to create a safe place for myself where I could escape. I knew I couldn't believe him anymore. I wrestled with the idea of divorce once again. Our kids were older now and had their own lives. Why not just tell him to leave? But I still believed Mark was the talisman that helped prevent my panic attacks, and if he left, I couldn't make it. But if I stayed in our marriage, I'd be choosing to be with a man who was emotionally absent and physically impotent. I felt caught between two painful choices.

One oppressively hot day in late July, on our way to the business, we stopped by the post office to pick up our mail. I was driving, because Mark was scheduled to have another sleep evaluation that night and wasn't supposed to drive. He was cranky, in a bad mood. When I asked if there was any mail for me, he refused to answer. I shoved an Eva Cassidy cassette into the tape deck. "You'll remember me," she sang, as I turned up the volume, "among the fields of gold."

I don't want to talk about my health, or our marriage, or the business, he shouted over her voice. I don't want to listen to you analyzing everything.

As I turned up the music, he leaned over as if to strike me with his handful of letters. Before I could react, he opened the car door and jumped out. I was driving thirty miles an hour down a paved country road. Was he trying to kill himself? Terrified, I pulled off the asphalt and started to call 911. Then I saw him walking through the high grass. Cars were moving in both directions as he started to cross the road. I held my breath and watched as he turned and headed toward home. He'd never make it. It was too far and too hot. Besides, he had asthma. If he walked in front of a car or had a heart attack, what would I tell our kids—that I didn't care enough to go back after their father?

Turning the car around, I drove onto the shoulder several feet in front of him and parked. To my surprise, he got into the car and immediately looked out his window. I kept quiet and tried to remain calm as I drove. Mark didn't say a word and headed downstairs to his den as soon as we arrived home. I was uneasy about leaving him alone and thought back to 1987, when Dr. Taylor told him he needed to be hospitalized for depression. As far as I could tell, Mark had been depressed ever since he told me about his addiction, probably even earlier than that, and now he had sleep apnea and a heart arrhythmia to deal with as well. If he really wanted to commit suicide, he'd find a way. But today, after he jumped out of a moving car, I was frightened and phoned his psychiatrist, leaving a message about what happened. Mark had told me never to call her, but I felt it was important to let her know.

I knocked on Mark's door. Come in, he muttered. He was stretched out on his leather recliner, painstakingly studying his hands.

I'm going out to the business to see about the staffing and orders. I should be back in a few hours. Is there anything you need?

He shook his head.

I put a glass of water on his desk. Do you want me to leave the door open or closed?

Closed, he said. Shutting his eyes, he turned his face to the wall.

Once at the greenhouse, I fidgeted away the afternoon. The staff was busy with their chores, and I had no energy for my work. After an hour of wandering around, I left early and drove home. I wondered if Mark would be lying in a pool of blood or if I would find empty medicine bottles on the floor.

As soon as I arrived at the house, I checked the phone: no message from his therapist. Mark's car was still in the garage, but the house felt empty. I went downstairs to his den and knocked on his door. No answer. I knocked again—still no answer. I shouldn't have left him. Oh God, I thought, please don't let him be dead. I cracked open his door. His chair was empty.

As I hurried down the hall to Ethan's room, I heard the CPAP machine making its familiar *whish-wash* sound. The door was partway open and I looked in. Mark was lying on the bed, wearing his mask. Quietly, I backed out of the room. We'd both been very lucky that afternoon.

Mark and I were hooked together like a Chinese finger puzzle. We'd both hit bottom. He was strung out. Sleep apnea had taken a toll on him. Financially, his business was a wreck. As for myself, I felt beaten and scared. I prayed to God to give me the guts to go it alone.

Discovery

Without intimacy and sexual desire, all the emotional, physiological, and spiritual responses that comprise human sexuality couldn't be fully experienced within the marriage.

—*Amy Buxton*

Heat lightning flickered across the night sky. It was August: humid, with no breeze to ruffle the curtains, and too hot to sleep. Earlier that evening, I found Mark in the foyer outside our bedroom door making up the trundle bed. I asked what he was doing, and he said he wanted to be near me. I said it wouldn't work, that I'd still hear his machine. Besides, that bed would be uncomfortable, and he'd not sleep well.

As if to change my mind, he sighed. I've told you all my secrets. Maybe I should just be myself and not try so hard to please you. His face was drawn, and his beard needed trimming.

Exhausted and feeling the weight of all our thirty-five years together, all the different ways we'd struggled, I turned away. To do anything else is a lie, I said.

Gripping the banister, he quickly disappeared downstairs.

Restless and lonely, I prowled around the house, wanting reassurance that things could be all right after all and wondering if our children were fast asleep next to their loved ones. I stopped abruptly when an index card caught my eye—an 800 number was scrawled across it. Mark's computer had given him trouble earlier in the day; perhaps it was the Mac tech-support number. An ominous feeling came over me. I felt empty and cold, like the time Mark confessed he was a sex addict.

Pulling my silk kimono tightly around me, I sat down on my bed and dialed the number on the card. A seductive male voice answered. Welcome to cruising-for-sex.com. This site is for men like...... What? In a kind of shocked panic, I tore downstairs and pulled up the website on my computer. I stared in astonishment as images of naked men having sex unfolded on the screen. I slammed shut the computer and stumbled back to my bedroom, where I grabbed my phone and called the number again—this time I wanted the whole story. Welcome to cruising-for-sex.com, said the voice again. This is a dating phone line for guys like you. Hey stud, you can go to the back room; just put in your number and enter club leathers. The man's high-pitched whine feigned intimate delicacy.

The truth hit me. Mark was gay. So *that* was the secret he'd been keeping all these years. I remembered the weird dream I'd had back in '87—searching and not finding him. Of course I couldn't find him; he wasn't there. He had labeled himself a sex addict to put me off his trail. No wonder I felt amputated.

I walked into the bathroom and stared at myself in the mirror. You are one dumb kiddo, I said aloud as I slid down the wall and flopped in a heap. Pounding on the tile with my fists, I started to scream. How could I have been so stupid? Why didn't I know? I answered myself with the standard line. Because you didn't want to know.

But what about the dozen therapists we saw along the way? During our thirty-five years of marriage, not one of them had ever mentioned that Mark might have some gender-preference issues. Had they suspected it but decided not to discuss the possibility with us? Ethically speaking, that was a frightening thought. Or was Mark really a consummate actor? He had insisted he was a sex addict. Maybe he succeeded in convincing us all, even himself.

The night heat lifted, and it was raining. I gave myself the finger as I walked by the mirror. I couldn't stop swearing. I tore around our bedroom grabbing everything in sight—CDs, picture frames, books—and flung them across the room. We had vowed to stay together in sickness and in health, but I couldn't honor that any longer. Looking back, it was easy to see that Mark had hid behind his clerical collar. To that disguise he'd added a doctor's stethoscope. Having a wife and family completed his masquerade. I realized that Mark's decision to remarry was not only for his

love of Ethan, but also to meet his need for self-preser-
vation. Exhausted from my flood of rage, I sank down
on the bed, demoralized and beyond fury.

I wish he could have loved me enough to tell me
the truth. It would take several years for me to forgive
myself for the biggest mistake of my life: staying with
Mark after he disclosed his addiction in 1987. Back
then, I didn't think I could face my panic attacks alone,
and so I'd stayed, convincing myself the reason was
that Lexa needed two parents.

Should I go downstairs and tell him to leave? I hesitated and then phoned Ethan. He answered in a sleepy
voice and listened as I told him the current scenario.

I can't tell you what to do, Mom. All I know is
that you've taken more abuse over the years than any
person should have to bear.

How much did he know? I pitched Mark's pillow
across the room.

I wish there were something I could do. Ethan's
voice was calm.

There isn't. I just have to get him out. Thanks for
listening. I'll call you later—when it's really morning.
I sat very still as I readied myself to tell Mark to leave.
Pieces of the puzzle I had called my marriage slowly
began to fall into place. How could I be a whole woman
if I was married to a gay man?

I called my closest friend, Kris. She'd understand.
She'd had a difficult divorce herself some years ago. I
told her my decision.

Well, my dear, I think you've known for a long time
that this would happen, she said.

I figured our marriage was over. But I never knew he was gay. I heard myself moan. How could he have lied all those years?

He didn't want anyone to know, Kris explained. He didn't even want to admit it to himself. Being gay didn't fit the picture he'd created. So, what are you going to do now? Kris's steady voice calmed me. Do you think he'll try to hurt you?

I was glad she asked me. I remembered the one time he did beat me. It was in front of Ethan when he was only five. He ran after his father, crying, You have to say you're sorry, Daddy, you have to say you're sorry.

Mark never hit me again.

Speaking quickly into the phone, I answered Kris. I don't think so. He'll be mad as hell. His cover's blown now, but he's not a very physical person, I said as my eyes filled with tears.

If he's gay, why had he gone to bed with me, I asked myself. The thought of a gay man making love to a straight woman struck me as heartbreakingly poignant. No wonder he had never caressed my breasts or whispered to me when we made love.

I didn't realize it at the time, but I had already begun to detach. To stem my hurt, I stored my heart on a shelf and shriveled up inside. Emotionally abandoned, I gradually withdrew and entered a closet of my own.

Do you want me to come over? I can park out of sight, Kris said.

Her question interrupted my thoughts. Would you? I said. It'd be nice to have her as backup.

I can be there in seconds.

Give me twenty minutes. Then if you don't hear from me, call the police. Otherwise, I'll phone you when he's leaving. I stood up, steadier on my feet now, my mind a little clearer.

Are you sure?

Yes, I promise. I'll call soon, I said, searching my purse for some money. I pulled the car key off my keychain and stuck it in my pocket along with cash for cab fare and the index card for proof of my discovery.

Standing outside Mark's bedroom door, I had a fantasy of throwing a hand grenade into his room. I knocked. No response. Then in a muffled voice, I heard him mutter something.

As I opened the door, Mark pulled the CPAP mask from his face and groped for his glasses. Reaching for his machine, he flipped it off and sank back on his pillows. I thought I caught a smirk slip across his face.

It's time for you to leave now. I waved the 1-800 card in front of him. Does this number mean anything to you?

No!

What about the website cruising-for-sex.com?

His hair, wet from the moisture of his breathing machine, was plastered across his forehead. In slow motion, he rose up from the bed. I was ready to run if he made a move toward me. What do you want, he asked.

I told you. It's time for you to leave. I have some money for you and the phone numbers of taxis you can call.

I won't take a taxi. He started to take apart his CPAP machine.

Why not, I asked as I fumbled in my bathrobe pocket for the key and twenty-dollar bills.

Because I've got too much to pack.

I might have laughed if I hadn't been so mad. What on earth was he going to take in the middle of the night? My grandmother's dining-room table?

I won't go in a taxi, he repeated as he stood in front of the bed, the machine clutched to his chest.

Then take the SUV. Here's the key. Bring it back in twenty-four hours. I wanted him out.

He pulled his head into his shoulders like a box turtle. I was afraid he might not leave after all. Mark, it's Wednesday morning, I said. We already have an appointment with Dr. Perkin tomorrow. We could use a third party to—

I won't be there.

Then I'll get your duffle bag.

Upstairs, I pulled Mark's black overnight case off the shelf and called Kris from my bedside phone. She said she was already parked in our neighbor's driveway and told me to call her if I had any trouble.

Thank God, she was nearby. I was shaking, afraid Mark wouldn't really go; afraid I would end up in a ball of panic.

Here's your bag. I dropped it on the floor and returned to my bedroom to be near the phone. Minutes later, he trudged into our bathroom. I watched as he balanced his bag on the edge of the Jacuzzi, threw in some clothes, and swept the contents from his medicine cabinet into his suitcase. He had enough drugs to kill himself. I just wanted him out, not dead.

He zipped up his suitcase, clutched his CPAP kit, and sauntered down the hall. I wondered if I would miss the stranger I'd lived with for so many years. For a second he lingered in front of the garage door. I reached for the doorknob. Please, Mark, wait a minute.

Brushing my hand aside, he pulled open the door and walked toward the car. Then he turned slowly and started toward me. His jaw was set, his eyes narrow behind his rimless glasses. He looked snarly—so different from the man I'd married.

Mark, I'm sorry it has to be this way.

He slammed the door-opener switch, and I instinctively raised my arm to shield my face, remembering when he'd beaten me in front of Ethan. Spinning away from me, he marched to the car, threw in his bags, and backed out of the garage. The tires screeched as he pulled out of the driveway. I wasn't certain if I'd see him again.

Seconds later, Kris knocked at my side door. She stepped inside and shook the rain from her short blond curls. How long have you been standing guard, I asked.

Long enough to watch him peel down the road. Putting her arm around my waist, she steadied me as we walked to the kitchen sunroom.

My legs felt like rubber bands. I was wobbly and couldn't get my sense of balance. I sat down on the couch and began to rock back and forth. No tears came, just a moan from deep within me. I feel exposed, like a hermit crab without a shell, I said.

That makes sense. Your married life has been ripped away, Kris replied.

I grabbed her hand. I need someone to hold on to, I said. I don't know what's real anymore. Maybe it's all a mistake. If I just sit here and don't move, maybe everything will be okay. But I know that isn't true.

You're being bombarded now. I remember that from when my marriage collapsed. Everything seems to have fallen apart. You feel like you're hanging out in nowhere.

That sounds about right. I took a deep breath and suddenly began to shake.

I think you need some hot tea. She headed toward the stove. Or would you like a stiff drink?

I wouldn't mind the drink, but I feel a little woozy, so I'd better stick with the tea. I pulled a throw around my shoulders and curled into a corner of the couch.

Kris put the kettle on the stove to boil, and before I knew it, she was headed to the living room. I asked her what she was doing. I'll be on your sofa till morning, if you need me. She put the mug on the table in front of me. Then, touching my shoulder, she gave me a faint smile. No woman should be left alone in the middle of the night when she's just discovered her husband's gay and she's told him to leave the house. You're your own woman now. Welcome to the sisterhood.

Putting my nose to the lip of my cup, I drew in the sharp, sweet smell of hibiscus leaves. Suddenly I was aware of the space around me. The room seemed to be getting bigger, and I felt overwhelmed and very small. Questions were banging around in my head. What else had he been involved with that I didn't know about? How long had all this really been going on?

I curled up on my side of the bed, numb, empty, and alone in a very different way than before. My mind spun through past scenes filled with secrets and ambiguities. I tried to sort things out—what exactly had happened and why—but I didn't know where to begin. I thought of our children. Certainly, they would come home once they knew what had happened. They'd want to hear both sides of the story.

The night was ending when I phoned Ethan again and told him that his dad had left. He said he'd grab a flight and be in Madison before midnight. Relieved that I'd see him soon, I called Lexa, who was living in Arizona. When I explained what had happened, she started to cry. I wanted to hold her in my arms. The truth was, I wished she were holding me. I reassured her that everything would work out okay, but of course, I didn't have a clue. I just wanted out. Was it possible that Mark was a gay sex addict? Nothing much made sense anymore.

The faint gray of early morning hovered around the kitchen curtains. The cuckoo clock on the wall reminded me it was almost six. A thought occurred to me as I hunted for the coffee can. In 1975, the time Mark claimed to have started visiting hot johns, openly gay men were not being ordained in the Episcopal Church. He would have risked more than controversy if he had admitted his sexual preferences then. But by remaining closeted, he had been false to everyone: not just his children and me, but to his church and his friends.

As I started the coffee, Mark's usual chore, I thought about all the pills he had taken with him. I knew he didn't want me to talk with his psychiatrist, but I called her later in the day anyway. Her chilling response was that his pills were none of my business. What an insensitive woman. If he takes his life, it'll be on your shift then, not mine, I said before I hung up on her. No matter what he had done, he was still my children's father.

I was staring out the window when Kris walked into the room. You were up all night, weren't you? She put her arms around me, and I sank gratefully into her embrace.

Yes. I couldn't sleep.

That too will pass. Exercise will help. She grabbed her tote bag. I have to get to work, but I have my cell phone with me. Your new life is beginning now. Remember, you gave me the key to your home fifteen years ago, when I was struggling with my divorce. It made all the difference in my life, even though I never used it. Now I can give you a different kind of key. Call me this afternoon. I want to know how you're doing.

Kris, I can't thank you enough. My shoulders relaxed as a rush of gratitude washed over me. I realized I'd been holding my breath.

You already have. Don't forget to check in. If you don't phone, I'll come by. I still have your key, she said. She waved as she walked out the side door.

❧

It wasn't until later, after Ethan and Lexa had come

and gone, that I went into hiding and hung around the house. I was having a hard time sleeping at night, and I didn't have much appetite. Kris often stopped by and insisted that I needed to walk with her. I said I couldn't. A month passed before I let her drive me to the walking trail near our homes. I wrapped my arms around myself. I don't know if I can walk very far, I said. Putting her hand firmly on the small of my back, she told me to put one foot in front of the other. I resisted her like a recalcitrant child. It was slow going at first, and I complained bitterly.

One late-fall day, when all but the most determined oaks had lost their leaves, Kris and I were taking a walk. Suddenly I stopped in my tracks. I know what I want, I said. But I don't think I'll find it right away. Wherever I land and with whom, it won't be out of fear, but out of choice and commitment.

I'll be there with you when you do, she promised. And she was.

Preparing for Divorce

But somewhere between understanding and
forgiveness there is another wall too wide to
get around.

—*Rick Bragg*

When I arrived for my appointment with Dr. Perkin,
her office door was open. I went in, chose my favorite
stuffed chair, and tucked my legs under me, feeling
small and safe. For more than two years, Mark and I
had a standing appointment with her on Wednesdays,
but I wasn't expecting him now after what we had said
to each other early that morning. Mark isn't coming
today, I said. There's a problem. I described what had
happened, that I discovered Mark was gay. He said he
wouldn't be here. You know how punctual he is, so I
guess he really meant it.

I'd scarcely finished my story when Mark sauntered
in and took his usual spot on the couch. Steadying my

voice, I tried to rein in my fury. Do you want to be in an honest, healthy, and whole marriage with me? I waited for his answer. I thought it was important for our therapist to hear it too. It didn't seem possible that we could stay together. But in spite of my contempt, after thirty-five years it was hard to face the final break.

No, was his prompt reply.

Then you can leave, because Dr. Perkin and I have lots to discuss.

He sat silently, swinging his leg back and forth. Several minutes passed. Suddenly he turned to me and said, You're a rage-filled person, and I don't want to be caught in your anger anymore.

You seem pretty pissed yourself today, Mark, Dr. Perkin shot back. She was a small, slim woman.

I am. He nodded, folding his arms across his chest.

Perhaps you should tell Gale what you *do* want, since you indicated you do not want to stay in your marriage.

After opening his briefcase, he pulled out a yellow legal pad and began to read from his notes. He announced that we were to live apart for six months and meet twice weekly to discuss his business matters, our home, and our children. He thought we should each work with our own counselor, instead of together with Dr. Perkin. Then, after the six months, he wanted us to conference with Dr. Perkin, at which time she would assess if we were ready to continue our marriage.

I wasn't certain what six months would do for him, but I knew it didn't suit my plans. I had interviewed two divorce lawyers in early July, right after throwing my wedding ring at him. I was furious about the porn and livid that I had been deceived. I needed to buy some time to sort out my next move, but I knew I couldn't live with an imposter anymore.

Mark paused and adjusted his glasses. Frowning at me, he said, After a few months, I might want to have a date with you.

That was a lie. He just wanted to continue using me as a cover. I wanted to yell, We're ending a marriage here! God, can't you help? Had Mark forgotten the gay website I discovered? I wasn't going to let him provoke me, so holding on to my fury, I uncurled myself and placed both feet firmly on the floor.

Looking at Mark, Dr. Perkin continued, You see this separation time as a step to divorce, then? She took off her horn-rimmed glasses and held them in her hand.

Maybe. I don't know really. Perhaps we could work with you sometime later, as I said, to see if we might be ready to resume our marriage. Mark shot a glance at me. Of course, you'd stay in the house, he said. But I'll need some money for an apartment and living expenses.

I must have been sitting there with my mouth open.

All my money is in the business, he said.

He wasn't making any sense. We're talking about the end of our marriage—I was the wrong sex for him—but maybe he would want to date sometime? And he wanted me to pay for his room and board somewhere? Perhaps I was naïve before, but not now. Wanting to sound reasonable, I squelched my anger, but it seeped into my voice as I leaned forward and said, The real issue is that you've been having sex with men for years, and you're hooked on porno and cybersex as well. Our marriage doesn't have a chance.

Before I could say anything else, Dr. Perkin intervened with a question. Mark, I assume you've been working with your own counselor on your gender issues. No, I'm not. He leaned back on the couch, looking calmer now that he had made his delivery.

Well, what have you been working on?

What I want to do with the rest of my life, he replied, rapidly tapping the sofa arm with his pencil.

I see. I gather you've told Gale the number of male contacts you've had over the years—several hundred. She studied his face. Considering that Gale's the only woman you've been sexually intimate with, I'm inclined to say that you're gay. I believe my colleagues would come to the same conclusion. That's an issue that needs addressing if you're in a marriage with a straight woman.

Well, I'm *not* gay. He shook his head as if to confirm this with himself.

I was grateful to hear Dr. Perkin's reply. I wasn't surprised by Mark's answer. He was being confronted, and he didn't like it.

What would you say your gender orientation is, then, she said, running her fingers through her dark, curly hair.

Maybe I'm bisexual, he offered curtly.

I opened my daily planner and wrote out "what will bisexuality do for me?" I answered my own question, writing "nothing" in large letters. I had made my decision: divorce was my next step. I just didn't know how to go about it. Feeling somewhat shaky, I stood up and said, I'll let you know what I think of your plan at our next meeting.

On the way home, I tried to get my head around Mark's sexuality claims. As I sorted through our lives together, what had evolved became clearer to me: I was married to a quick-change artist, and I had missed all the signs.

When I got home, I phoned Dr. Perkin. He's gay, isn't he? I wanted her confirmation.

Well, he came close to admitting he has a gender-preference issue when he said he might be bisexual.

I think his so-called sexual addiction is a cover for his homosexuality. I think he uses it so he doesn't have to admit he's gay. Holding the phone, I walked across the kitchen and slumped down on the couch.

That's certainly possible. Perhaps a separation time will give him some space to figure that out.

I'm not interested in hanging around for him to catch on, I said. The tears I had fought all day spilled out now, as I began to grasp how thoroughly he'd used me. It doesn't matter if Mark's gay or bisexual, I said. There's no point in my staying married to him. I wish he'd told me. God knows I tried to reach out to him, but he wasn't there. He was buried in the bottom of the closet.

That does seem to be the case. Go easy on yourself. This is a difficult time. I'll see you next week. Call me if you need to, she said.

Thanks. I have to learn to manage somehow. I put

down the phone, picked up the Kleenex box, and flung it across the room. I'd been Mark's wife for thirty-five years—didn't that count for *anything?* I found our wedding album and began pulling out the photos. I cut Mark's face out of every picture, methodically at first— an ear, then his beard, and finally his hand, which was holding mine. Sometimes I simply sliced off his head. When I finished, I closed the album and put it back on the shelf. Then I scooped up the fragments of our past and fed them to the shredder.

Ethan and Lexa both arrived in Madison midafter-noon the following day. They met with their father to hear his side of the story. Ethan told me later that he made certain Mark told Lexa about his sexual addic-tion. She came home in tears, packed an overnight bag, and spent the night with Cathy, her best friend from high school. That evening Ethan helped me fill out some forms that my attorney had requested. The next afternoon the children and I had an appointment with Dr. Perkin. After she summarized what their dad and I been struggling with, she asked to speak to the two of them alone.

During dinner that evening, they told me she'd sug-gested that they each have a few sessions with a coun-selor. That helped ease my concerns, and as far as I could tell, they seemed more relaxed. Ethan, Lexa, and I should have talked about what had happened, but we didn't. At the time, I felt it was too painful and awkward to discuss. It would be years before any of us mentioned it, even in the abstract. We went about our lives, careful to avoid mentioning the death that had occurred in our family.

Ethan and Lexa left at the end of the week, and I stopped working in Mark's greenhouses. I missed the camaraderie with the staff. I said good-bye to all of them and took a last look at all the flowers I had taken care of during the past ten years.

During those early weeks of being separated, I slogged through the days, feeling the viciousness of shame and disgust. I had trouble navigating around corners and bruised myself when I bumped into table edges and doorjambs. How would I ever explain to my friends what had happened to us? I shopped late at night, when the grocery store was nearly empty. I was calmer then and seemed to have more control over my anxiety. As a nurse, I knew how to care for others, but I wasn't very good at asking for help for myself. I thought I could manage everything on my own, when it was obvious to others that I couldn't.

Only a few days had passed, although it felt like a century, when my phone rang at dinnertime. Hello, I said cautiously, uncertain about anyone entering my space.

It's me, Andrew. Sally and I haven't seen you around. What's up?

Oh, nothing really. Thoughts raced through my head—had they heard, I wondered.

You sound a little down.

Andrew was a lawyer. He and Sally were good friends of ours. Should I tell them? I took a deep breath and started in. Well, I guess I am, a little. You won't believe this but...and then I quickly told him what had happened.

You need to get ahead of this thing. This is what I would do, he said. Call up a dozen of your closest friends and tell them the story. They need to hear it from you before rumors start going around. People will want to help.

Okay, I said. I respected his opinion. But—

No buts. It's important.

Although I felt mortified, I did what he suggested. None of my friends ever asked me what happened; they seemed to already know. Several friends stopped by to visit; others invited me to dinner and didn't say anything when I arrived without Mark. A year later, Andrew told me that the rumor mill never got started. I was grateful for his advice and counsel.

The days were getting shorter, and the maple leaves were turning the color of ripe plums. The evenings cooled, and I felt loneliness creeping up on me. In order to get some hold on my anxiety, I arranged to have one of my friends stay at my house during the next three months. I knew I had to wean myself off that arrangement, but it was tough going. It was late October before I got the guts to go solo. The first night alone I stayed awake until morning, just to keep away the old ghosts.

Time stretched in odd directions that fall of 2000. My days were like veiled sunsets, beginning at the end of the day. I couldn't sleep, and I couldn't sit still. I roamed through the house, recalling the times we'd spent together. We built a family, and now I was left in solitude to dismantle it, inventorying our marriage as I divided up our things. One night I climbed up the kitchen ladder and grabbed the green glazed clay bowl on the top pantry shelf. Friends, both ceramicists, had made it for us and inscribed our wedding date on the bottom. I don't need that memory, I thought, and with a great deal of satisfaction, I dropped it off the back deck. It splintered magnificently. I spent a lot of time that autumn picking up breakage on the back lawn.

Afraid that Mark might come by, every evening I made certain the windows were closed and the doors locked. The house was always silent, no music or other sounds but the *tap tap* of the cats' paws padding down the hallway. Occasionally my Bengal cat, Saucer, would rub against my legs, begging me to play. For a few moments, I would forget my isolation as I stroked her tummy and burrowed my head in her fur, but soon the reality of everything would catch up to me, and I would feel torn between my grief and vengeance. Who was I now? The not-quite-divorced woman of a married man who never wanted a wife? He had conned me, leaving me furious to have been so stupid, to have been fooled, to have believed him.

I usually went to bed at two or three in the morning, after rummaging through birthday cards, love letters and poems, and the detritus of decades, pondering over all our history, tearing it up and throwing it away. Then, early one morning, while the dawn was fingering its way across our nature lake, I found a large white box labeled "Wedding Dress" in the guest room closet.

I carried it to the living room and set it down in front of the fireplace. I felt I was bringing a sacred item to an altar. I ripped open the box and stared at the folded silk organza. When I last wore the dress, I was a young woman joined together with a man to make a marriage and conceive children.

That night I wondered if Mark ever thought about what might have transpired had he told me the predicament he was in. I wondered if he had ever thought of taking me into his confidence. I doubted I would ever learn the answers to my questions.

The fire had been built. All I had to do was strike a match and touch the nearest pinecone. The logs burst into flame. For a moment, I stared at my gown, replaying that glorious day in San Francisco. Then, taking a deep breath, I grabbed the dress, held it close for a second, and tossed it into the crackling fire. A sickening power shuddered through me as I watched it disappear in the flames, a brown singe spreading slowly across the skirt. Soon all that remained were hot ashes.

When I married Mark, I was ready to share my whole self with him—mind, body, and soul—but now I knew he had not really wanted me. I remembered how he once described our marriage as distance within intimacy. Perhaps he'd been trying to tell me something then. Too late now. Burning my wedding dress marked an end to the marriage I'd held on to for so many years.

During the next few weeks, I hunkered down and muddled through trying to get used to eating alone, even if it was only half a TV dinner. One day, my brother stopped by during his annual visit to our parents' graves and was shocked when I showed him Mark's office. He stared in amazement at the piles of stuff filling the room. You mean he kept his business and your joint expenses in this mess? My brother's comment was a wake-up call. During our marriage, I had become accustomed to Mark's unmanageable chaos. For years, I worked to sidestep the turmoil I lived in and in doing so, I avoided dealing with my own challenges and failings.

Now my life would be different, but I had no idea what obstacles lay just in front of me. Friends visited from time to time, but in my distraction, I felt distant from them. Like a puppet on a string, I would nod my head, converse politely, and thank them for coming. I should have worn a long black dress, like a widow receiving guests in the parlor while everyone dutifully makes small talk. Occasionally I would touch my naked ring finger, feeling the dent where my wedding band had been for so many years, wishing there could have been a different ending.

9

Clerics

Admitted to God, to ourselves, and to another human being the exact nature of our wrongs.
>—*The Fifth Step, Alcoholics Anonymous Twelve-Step Program*

Mark never lived in our house again. He stopped by to pick up some of his belongings, but it wasn't until mid-October that he showed the movers what to pack. My friend Rachel spent the day at my house and made me stay in the kitchen while Mark directed the men. When his furniture, filing cabinets, and family portraits were gone and half our joint clothes closet emptied, the house looked abandoned and untidy. Walking through the rooms, checking to see exactly what he'd taken, I found a floppy disc on the floor of his study and put it in my pocket. The only things that still needed dividing up were our music collection and our books. The CDs and old records would be easy, but the books would take much longer. As I stood in the middle of our living room, I knew I wanted to sell the house. It was too big, and the memories it held were more than I could face.

One rainy, cold day in early November, I dragged myself down to the basement library where Mark and I stored many of our books. As I pushed open the heavy door, I almost knocked over a tower of empty cardboard cartons. A small blue Tiffany box balanced on top of the arrangement; inside it was a black leather Bible with a bundle of papers tucked in its fold. It looked as though someone had worked carefully to create a display. Puzzled, I grabbed the bunch of papers and began to read. "Fifth Step" was typed at the top of the first page. I figured it was most likely something from a twelve-step program. Having attended the COSA twelve-step program years ago, I knew that the fifth step meant telling your group exactly what you'd done.

My hands shook as I started to read Mark's detailed descriptions of his sexual contacts. I tried to skip over some of the details, but words jumped out at me: *I masturbated men who were as young as (probably) thirteen and as old as seventy.* Stunned, I read it again just to be sure. Children? That was *illegal*! Scared as hell, I ran up the stairs with the statement in my hand. I knew I should report what I had read. Dropping the papers on the kitchen counter, I reached for the phone.

I needed to call someone with authority—I'd start with the bishop. As an Episcopal priest, Mark would have to answer to his bishop. Filled with dread, I called the diocese and asked to be connected with the bishop's secretary. I explained that I was married to one of the priests in the diocese and had a clerical emergency. I used the phrase "oxford files"—the password my church used to refer to inappropriate clergy behavior—and demanded to see the bishop immediately. In a muffled but urgent tone, the person on the line consulted someone and then told me to come in at one that afternoon.

I tried to sort out what should be done. Weren't clergy required to notify the authorities about sexual abuse? Or should I? As a licensed registered nurse, I knew about reporting laws. I phoned my divorce attorney for her advice. Let your bishop handle it, she said quickly.

Should I let him read the document?

Absolutely, but don't leave it with him. He can have a copy for his files when your divorce is finalized. You should be getting the decree next month, hopefully before Christmas.

Lightheaded, I hung up the phone, and unable to keep my balance, I grabbed for the nearest kitchen chair to steady myself. I shuddered as I skimmed over Mark's paper—pages filled with painstaking accounts of his exploits and emotional suffering—his bitterness, fears, and anger. How wretched that we both had lived side by side aching in loneliness, unable to reach out to one another. As I turned the pages, I realized how Mark had maneuvered me into initiating the divorce he always wanted but never asked for. How could I have shared a bed with him all those years, held him in my arms, had his children? Now I understood that I hadn't known him. I felt naked and more defiled than before.

I phoned Rachel and asked her if she'd drive me into Madison to see the bishop. The dark clouds were getting larger, and I was shaky and afraid to drive by myself. On our way, as I gathered my courage, I told her some of the shocking things that I'd discovered in Mark's testimony. Most people would be horrified, I thought, and it was a relief to hear her express it.

That's really appalling, Rachel exclaimed. Your bishop will have to report him. There are rumors about those things in the Roman Church. I quit that church long ago, but I can't see how your bishop would let him continue as a priest—not with all that information. By the way, the day the movers came...Rachel paused, then taking a deep breath she said, I found a magazine that was left behind, meant for the trash, I guess. I saw nude men in it. I brought it with me—you need to give it to the bishop.

I guess that shouldn't surprise me, I said and then continued on. There were naked men on the website I saw back in August. I was silent after that as I remembered the floppy disc I'd found on the floor of Mark's room the day the moving van came to take pack up his belongings. I'd have to review it when we got home. I wondered how often bishops were faced with situations like mine.

The rain that started earlier had turned to snow as Rachel drove the car into the diocesan parking lot. The road would be icy before we got home. I shivered and pulled my coat tightly around me, wondering what would happen next.

We were ushered into the well-appointed diocesan waiting room. Almost immediately, the bishop arrived—a tall, imposing figure with a distinctive flair. His dark hair was full and streaked with silver. He wore a black suit, white clerical collar, and magenta shirt— the color reserved for bishops. He touched a large gold cross that was displayed prominently on his chest and held out his hand to me.

My room is just down the hall, he said as he nodded in the direction for me to proceed. I looked over my shoulder at Rachel and saw her give me a thumbs-up as I started toward the hallway. The bishop's office was generous; large windows framed the magnificent oak trees that surrounded the city park below. Artifacts and crucifixes from several countries were displayed in museum-style cabinets. One entire wall held a stunning number of leather-bound books, but I was more scared than impressed. He invited me to make myself comfortable. Feeling like the smallest bird at the feeder, I perched on the edge of a massive couch while he drew up a chair across from me. Reaching for a legal pad, he said, You don't mind if I take notes, do you?

Not at all, I replied. I had expected him to. As if it were contaminated, I handed him the bag containing the magazine. He flipped through a few pages. It's just gay porn, he said.

Just gay porn, I thought to myself. Was he used to seeing gay porn? He didn't even grimace. I couldn't believe the bishop's nonchalant response. I wanted to shake him. Don't you get it? Mark's married to me, and I am a heterosexual woman, but instead I said calmly, I'd like you to read the document that I discovered today. I handed him the thirteen typed pages I found in the Bible. Mark left this in our home when he moved out, I explained. After you read it, I think you'll understand why I needed to see you.

He reached for his glasses and skimmed through the disclosure, pausing several times to take notes. I sat motionless, trying to read his face. By reputation, he was aloof and distant, not at all like warm and friendly Bishop Pike, who had performed our marriage ceremony. Was he crafting some kind of plan as he read?

A half hour later, he took off his glasses and turned toward the windows. After I've written up my notes, may I e-mail them to you? I'll need you to review them for accuracy: dates, names, and anything else that needs clarity. You can e-mail them back to me when you're finished. He leaned back stiffly in his chair. Only my chancellor and secretary will see them. An uncomfortable silence filled the room.

Nodding yes, I waited for him to say that he was sorry for what we both now knew, sorry for the boys who had been exploited by my priest husband. Didn't he care? Was that it? Perhaps I was supposed to leave. I sat quietly, my hands folded, trying to keep calm. I didn't want him to be upset with me. I didn't want to appear aggressive. I might need his assistance in the future, and I didn't want to alienate him now. I was intent on delivering this shocking information, and, as my attorney suggested, I expected him to act on it.

I imagined that as the pastor of his flock, he'd try to console me or at least show some concern for our children and even for Mark, but he simply told me I should see a spiritual counselor. Wasn't *he* supposed to be a spiritual counselor? I needed someone to tell me everything would be all right—to tell me it wasn't my fault—but I sensed he wasn't going to be that comforting person.

While I sat listening to what he didn't say, I began to make some decisions. Soon my divorce would be final, but now I believed that it wouldn't establish the total detachment from Mark that I desired. I wanted an annulment. The Episcopal Church didn't have annulments in the same way that the Roman Catholic Church did, but there had to be something comparable. I needed my whole person to be spiritually and physically separated from Mark in the most official way possible in the eyes of my church. I wanted to be considered a single woman, not a divorceé. My first prayer as I sat there in my bishop's office was that this nightmare had never happened—to any of us, even the people I would never know.

I stood up, swung my purse over my shoulder, and turned to face the bishop. I want the equivalent to an annulment, I said. I want the church's sanction that I have no relationship with this man.

Pulling himself erect, he said, I'll have to talk with Mark first.

What? He would ask my soon-to-be ex-husband—

who had violated his marital and priestly vows—to weigh in on my status in the church? What kind of a two-tiered system was this? My face grew hot, and I tightened my grip on my bag but didn't move an inch.

He mentioned something about how much courage it took me to come to him, and then he bowed his head, mumbling some kind of prayer, but it held nothing for me. It appeared that the bishop was more preoccupied with how Mark's situation would reflect on his diocese than his concern about my children or me.

It was late afternoon when I got home, and the sky was filled with heavy clouds. I sat for a long time looking at soft snow filling in the branches of our evergreens. Should I call child protective services? No. My lawyer had told me to let the bishop deal with the problem of child abuse. I felt caught in a dark labyrinth, faced with dead ends and no options. My church had abandoned me. My body started to tremble. God help me. God help all of us, I whispered half-heartedly, feeling that maybe God had checked out too.

As I tried to make some plans, I thought back to the August morning when I had told Mark to leave. I knew we were headed for divorce and called my parish priest to talk it over. I didn't want to be hasty about breaking my vows and wanted his assistance in sorting it out, but he told me he didn't have any time that week. I hung up, surprised at his attitude, at his lack of support, and at his failure to offer any kind of help. Later I learned that his wife was ill, but I thought divorce was something a priest would take seriously.

He had dismissed me, and now it seemed the bishop had done the same thing.

Filled with energy that had no place to go, I paced around the kitchen and headed downstairs to the guest-room. Opening the closet door, I pulled off the bed sheet protecting the heavily gold-embroidered chasuble—the cape priests wear over their vestments. I had purchased it for Mark's graduation from medical school in 1972, when he was to give the benediction for his graduating class. I remembered how pleased and proud he looked as he walked to the podium—tall and handsome in his flowing green-velvet robe.

Mark had worn his chasuble when he performed Ethan and Angela's wedding ceremony in 1993, but now he would never wear it again. I marched upstairs with the heavy robe in my arms, intent upon my mission. I made a small fire and fed it with newspaper, but it was slow to start. The burning wood smelled stale and moldy, perhaps from the rain that had dripped down the flue. Folding the robe in half, I stuffed it into the fire. Instead of bursting into flames, it produced thick smoke that fill the chimney. I poked and prodded until the fire began to feed on the fabric. I prayed for forgive-ness as if I were committing some horrible crime, but I needed some way to obliterate Mark's presence and destroy symbolically everything he'd done to deceive and hurt others and myself. He no longer had the right to wear clerical attire. Maybe the bishop didn't under-stand that yet, but I did.

As I sat in front of the fire, I searched for some way to work through what had happened with the bishop.

Due to Mark's position as a priest, I knew a number of clergy, and some of them were bishops. I decided to call Porter, a bishop who was married to a close friend of mine. I trusted him. Porter answered the phone. I told him about my visit with the bishop and that I'd burned a lot of Mark's clerical garments. When I finished, I said, I'm used up. I'm alone at the bottom of a pit.

I'm not surprised. You must feel you've been betrayed three times: first by your husband, then by the church, and of course by God.

That's about it, I think. But what am I going to do?

His voice was soft and compassionate. I want to think this all over for a few days, but first I want you to know you've done the right thing. Your bishop needs to handle this problem. It's flagrant professional misconduct, and it's complicated. Of course, each diocese is a little different. This case is in process now, and it can't be ignored. After pausing for a moment, he went on. I want you to be in touch with someone who's not a priest but who's working in the field of clergy misconduct. I think if you share what has happened, you'll get some helpful information on what the church is trying to do—not always swiftly, but trying.

From the way my bishop acted, I don't think our church cares, I said. I wanted to feel relieved, but I was still bewildered.

Oh no. It cares very much, but like any big institution, it has a hard time getting organized around such a loaded subject. But for you personally, my dear, right now I want you to have someone to confide in—not just anyone, but someone who's specially trained in this field. I need to make some inquiries, and I'll get back to you.

I've tried praying—nothing comes really. I keep saying, Give me courage, *please,* just give me courage.

There's nothing wrong with that, and I want you to know that I'll be praying for you,

After I hung up the phone, I leaned back in my chair. Dusk hovered over the lake. I felt encouraged by what Porter told me and not so terribly alone.

For the next few weeks, I was on a roller-coaster ride—one day I'd feel encouraged, certain I was going to get through this, and the next day I would be heavy with sorrow and self-loathing. My emotions weren't predictable. I felt that I was skidding downhill and made a call to a friend, a longtime parishioner at my church, and told her how I had tried to approach our rector. I know what you mean, she told me. You might try the priest at the little church by the creek in town. I've found her very helpful in the past. She's our age. The next week on my way home from shopping, I took her suggestion and stopped by the church. Earlier that day, I had learned that our divorce papers were filed, and I felt erased.

The distinct smell of old wood filled the air as I opened the doors of the small building. Hearing a keyboard's rapid *tat-tat-tat,* I headed in that direction and saw a woman wearing a clerical collar and a gray blouse, sitting behind a computer screen.

You look as though you need someone to talk to. She smiled and stood up. She wore her coal-black hair in a casual french twist, looking more like a movie star than a priest. My name's Caitlin. Would you like to walk around?

As we strolled through a long hallway to a library, I spilled my story, my session with the bishop, and how I tried to contact my rector. She listened to me intently, nodding her head from time to time. When I hesitated, she put her arm around me and gave me a hug that felt genuinely warm. As we returned to the vestibule I said, You know what? Our church doesn't do a very good job with divorce.

You're right. We don't do well in that department.

But isn't it places like that in our lives, the painful times, when the church would want to be there?

Yes, indeed, but people in general don't like to hang around pain. It makes them uneasy, she said softly, taking my hand.

I thanked her for listening to me and asked if I could attend services at her church. Of course. Think of us as an umbrella in a rainstorm. She stopped in front of the church doors. I'd like you to keep in touch with me.

The following Sunday I arrived at her church in plenty of time for the eight o'clock service. Not wanting to be noticed, I sat several rows back from the altar and off to one side. There were only a dozen people in the nave, and Caitlin, who was standing behind the altar, opened her arms wide and said, Like we always do, friends, please feel free to gather 'round. Still feeling uncertain, I joined the group and warily walked forward.

I was mad at my bishop and rector, but not really at God. This simple service, passing the common cup and eating homemade bread, connected me again to a ritual that always had made me feel better. There is something about standing with others at the communion rail that makes my eyes well up with tears, giving me a feeling of total acceptance, a sense of grace. It softens my self-criticism.

From then on, I attended the Sunday morning eight o'clock at Caitlin's church. The small group, which stood together during the brief homily and communion service, welcomed me into their circle. I needed to hear the words, God have mercy on you, strengthen you in all goodness—the peace of the Lord be always with you. I needed to say aloud, Forgive us our sins, as we forgive those who sin against us. I was having difficulty with forgiveness—a concept that would take me a long time to understand.

At Thanksgiving that year, I went to my friend Emily's house, but in spite of all the people and festivities, I was desolate. For the first time in thirty-five years, I was not celebrating with my family.

I thought back to the one other time I was alone at Thanksgiving—when I was pregnant with Deborah. I had walked to a twenty-four-hour store on University Avenue in Berkeley and bought myself a frozen chicken pie. When I returned to my apartment, I wasn't hungry. Now, years later, I had no appetite either and pushed the turkey and green beans about on my plate, trying to hide them under the silverware. I watched as Emily's husband ambled around the large table, stopping to talk with guests, filling our champagne glasses. He paused by Emily's chair and lightly touched her cheek. In response, she reached out and caressed his hand. I envied the loving glances they exchanged, aware that I had never even approached that kind of marriage.

As I watched couples interact that evening, I realized I had missed a lot in my marriage. I don't think Mark ever cherished me as a woman. Maybe that was why I felt so lonely even when he was with me. Then I had a piercing thought: Was I a constant reminder to Mark that he was gay?

It was dark and beginning to sleet when I left my friends' home later that night. The road was slippery, and I inched along carefully. Again, I blamed myself for not following my intuition that morning long ago when I asked Mark if he was gay. Would my experience of womanhood have been different if he'd been straight? Peering into the whirling snow, I wondered just how much I had lost.

The garage door opened as I drove up to the house, parked the car, and walked into the house. I headed toward the kitchen and suddenly felt panicky. I struggled for a deep breath of air and began to hyperventilate. Before I could brace myself, I was trembling in the rush of a massive anxiety attack. I tried to control my dizziness, tried not to think about dying. I sank to the floor. It was almost an hour before my breathing returned to normal, leaving me worn out and ragged with fear. I didn't want to be alone anymore. I was afraid the panic attacks would kill me. I had to do something differently, but I had no idea what. Hoping that Ethan was at home out in California, I picked up the phone and dialed his number.

Ethan, I'm sorry to bother you. I've just had another anxiety attack. I don't think I can go on like this much longer. I know I keep calling you and...

He gave a little chuckle, and immediately I felt relieved. Mom, Angela thinks you ought to come out here for a while. She says we're spending so much time on the phone that it'd be easier if you were here. There are lots of apartments nearby. I drew a deep breath of relief. The next evening Ethan arrived in Madison. I had already started to pack.

Welcome to LA

We hesitate, in the face of change, because
change is loss. But if we don't accept some
loss...we can lose everything.

—*Stephen Grosz*

A few days later, as the morning sun began to sparkle
on the frozen snow, Ethan and I climbed into a rental
SUV filled with everything I might need for a winter
in Southern California. As we drove away, I turned
my back on the house where I had lived with Mark
for almost twenty years. Ethan drove south toward
Kansas, where we would pick up the train in Topeka.
Leaning my head against the car window, I watched
snow-covered cornfields flashing by, stretching end-
lessly to the gray horizon. Fence posts blurred before
my half-closed eyes. My thoughts began to settle as my
body released the tension that had filled my life for so
many years: memories, scraps of dialogue, and feelings

from the years Mark and I had spent together. I wasn't certain what I'd left behind and had no idea what lay ahead.

We arrived just after midnight, turned in the car, boarded Amtrak's Southwest Chief for Los Angeles, and went directly to our adjoining sleeping compartments. No planes for me. I'd had a panic attack on a plane once and didn't want to chance it.

Exhausted by the long car trip, I fell asleep quickly. For the next six hours, the train sped through the Kansas grasslands. By morning, it was winding its way up Raton Pass into the high desert of Colorado, then down the other side, before racing through the red-rock canyons of New Mexico. I gazed out the dirty train window to see isolated herds of pronghorn antelope grazing on winter brush. We had yet to cross the Mojave Desert and wouldn't arrive in LA until the next afternoon.

After we got up and ate breakfast, we went back to our compartment. I looked at Ethan, who was engrossed in a science-fiction fantasy with his feet propped up on the windowsill, and said, I'm sorry I'm not a very entertaining traveling companion. I hardly have enough energy to look at the scenery. Did you sleep okay?

He looked up from his book and grinned. No problem, just like rocking in a cradle.

When I used to make this trip with your dad, I always listened to an audiobook and knitted at the same time. Sometimes I even wrote letters. But I don't want to do any of that today.

Well, Mom, maybe you did all that stuff to keep from looking at what you didn't want to see. Now that's over with.

Embarrassed and oddly uncomfortable, I shifted in my seat. Mmm, yes…that fits. How did you get to be so wise, anyway?

Just livin' and looking, I guess.

He raised his eyebrows and made a silly face. His solid, relaxed presence was a welcome relief. I'd forgotten what it was like to sit silently with someone I completely trusted. I felt no need to explain, apologize, or please. I only needed to be.

That night, as the train *click-clacked* along the tracks, my mind replayed past scenes. Shortly before I left Madison, I'd found a bunch of Mark's e-mails filed with our joint bank statements. They were dated 1990, the year of our twenty-fifth wedding anniversary. As I read the correspondence, it became apparent that Mark was involved in a lengthy association with a man in New York. They wrote about the possibility of meeting one another, but Mark explained it would be hard for him to get away. He gave my panic disorder as an excuse. One particular sentence pierced through me like Laertes's poisoned sword. In a poignant paragraph, Mark bared his soul, confessing that he was entrusting the "pearl" of his person to this man and that he had "no greater gift" to give. And all that time I thought he loved me.

As I lay on the narrow train berth, the solemn words of the Episcopal marriage ceremony echoed in my ears: *"I require and charge you both, as ye will answer at the dreadful day of judgment when the secrets of all hearts shall be disclosed, that if either of you know any impediment why you may not be lawfully joined together in Matrimony, ye do now confess it. For be ye well assured, that if any persons joined together otherwise than as God's Word doth allow, their marriage is not lawful."*

Had the love we professed for one another as we stood before the altar blinded us from the truth? Or was it the fear of societal shame that made us both feel like victims? We barely touched the surface of those emotions with one another. The truth was we both were cowards.

Pulling open the window curtain at the end of my bunk, I peered into the darkness. The train swayed rhythmically as we sped west through the night, across the high Arizona desert. As we rounded each bend, I watched the engine's searchlight seeking out strange forms in the night. The possibility that Mark might have tested positive for AIDS had brought me to my knees. Could I find the courage to reclaim myself? I wrapped the scratchy Pullman sheet around my shoulders and tucked myself into the corner to watch the sunrise as it began to inch across a rose-gold California sky.

I thought about another early winter morning when I stopped to visit my mother. She was near the end of her life, and getting up from bed consumed most of her energy. After she pushed herself to a sitting position, she struggled for a few breaths. Then, pounding her fist on the mattress, she shouted at herself, Elizabeth Anne, get out of your bed! And she did, each day until early one November morning when she didn't wake up. If she could find the strength to continue day after day, then so could I.

That next morning we arrived in Los Angeles. I had left behind greenhouses overflowing with luxuriant tropical plants and arrived in crowded, gritty LA. I only knew three people who lived in the city: my son, Ethan; his wife, Angela; and my friend Madeline, my eighth-grade boarding-school roommate, whom I hadn't seen in over forty years. Why did it seem that leaving home was a good idea?

During my first week in LA, I stayed at Angela and Ethan's before moving into a furnished apartment rented from a mutual friend. Her Toyota Highlander sat in the garage, ready for me to use. I felt as though I had just moved into a college dorm but had misplaced my "welcome to college" manual. Most nights, instead of staying in the apartment, I slept on an inflatable mattress on the floor of Ethan's home office. Feeling unsettled and tense in the dark room, I knew I was experiencing more than culture shock.

I spent my days at the apartment unpacking and settling in. I paced around, putting a stack of books in one corner and then an hour later moving them to another corner. I was relieved to have the company of my two cats, who had traveled out by cargo plane. They claimed the thin rays of sunlight slanting through the sliding-glass panels at the far end of the narrow living area. I hadn't lived alone in an apartment since before I was married, and I was disorganized and at loose ends. I wrote and rewrote lists of things to do. I had brought a few of my weaving projects with me, but after a few phone calls I concluded there wasn't anything like an art center nearby where I could rent a loom. What was I going to do with all my time?

Before I left Wisconsin, my doctor had recommended that I walk the beach every day until I was tired, so shortly after my arrival, Ethan took me to the coast and walked with me along a wooden stairway that snaked its way down the steep hillside to the ocean. The setting was not what I had imagined. The beach was huge, stretching fifty feet to the water's edge. The sand was concrete gray, so different from Lake Superior's beautiful white sand. Here the shoreline was littered with noisy people and barking dogs. There were no pebbles to collect, no driftwood, only sad bits of plastic paper, bottle tops, and tired pieces of slimy brown kelp. I couldn't envision long, healing walks there. The expanse of ocean all the way to the horizon seemed so flat and far away.

I was trying to leave an eternity of sorrow behind me, but seeing the vastness of the ocean, I wondered how to recover my life and myself after losing so much time—thirty-five years—married to the wrong man. I couldn't shove memories into a filing cabinet or just throw them out. I was trapped between a past I didn't like and a future I didn't know. At that time, 2000, the Internet wasn't as comprehensive as it is now, and I didn't know where to turn.

Since then, there has been a lot of discussion about the similarities between PTSD (post-traumatic stress disorder) and IRT (interpersonal relational trauma). A number of sites about sexual addiction are available with information and referrals. Now, women whose husbands have come out can find assistance in working through their concerns in online talk groups. And there are pages dedicated to how to work through anxiety issues. Even if these various sites are helpful only in assuring their readers that they are not alone in their dark nights, they have done a huge service.

At the end of the first week with my kids, I decided it was time to try being alone at night in the apartment. The elevator jiggled and took forever to arrive at my floor. I didn't like elevators; when I was a teen, I had a panic attack in one. But I had to take this one—it was the only way to get to the apartment. I missed my front door in Madison, where sweet autumn clematis twined around the porch trellises.

The rental apartment was painted an institutional white. It had two rectangular spaces: one for the kitchen and living area, the other for the bathroom and bedroom. When I sat down on the bed, I was reminded of Mark. I needed a different place to sleep. Each night I took my sheets and comforter from behind the couch and adjusted my pillows for reading or watching a movie on TV. My two cats—Meringue, the Siamese, and Saucer, the Bengal—slept like bookends on either side of me. In the morning, I folded up the bedclothes and stuffed them out of sight behind the sofa.

I'd only been there a few days when I locked myself out of my apartment, forgetting that I couldn't just go to the laundry room and back to my own kitchen without a key. From then on, I always carried my keys with me and hid them under my pillow at night. There were so many adjustments to get used to while trying to keep—or regain—my own equilibrium.

I believed I would be safe from an anxiety attack, at least in my apartment, and was able to manage the five-block drive to the grocery. I felt all right when I walked a half-block to rent DVDs. But when I had to drive the fifteen minutes to my son and daughter-in-law's after we started our weekly Wednesday suppers together, I was anxious all the way. I held on to my cell phone so that I could call them instantly if I needed to.

One morning, as I was getting dressed, I reached for a bottle of perfume—forgetting that I had tossed them all out before I left home. Afraid to go too far from my apartment alone, I asked Ethan to take me to the mall. He was as generous with his nose as he was with his time. He gagged on a few of the scents we tried. Blaggh, he said, sniffing a woody musk. A big, tall, heavy woman with a whole lot of moxie needs to wear this one. He laughed. I don't think it's you, Mom.

After several more sniffs, and the help of a patient young woman behind the counter who couldn't take her eyes off Ethan, we found a scent I liked, a Japanese floral spice with no powder hangover. It was on the market in time for Christmas. When I wore it, I started to make new memories.

Where next? he said with a grin.

I didn't want to take up too much of his time, but he convinced me that he wanted to keep shopping.

As we strolled along, I stopped for a moment to look at leather jackets hanging in a store window. Let's go inside, said Ethan.

Me, in a leather jacket. Are you kidding?

No, Mom, everyone wears them.

Not old ladies like me.

Mom, you don't look like an old lady. Besides, old ladies and old men wear them too.

I stroked some of the jackets; they were soft and buttery. I didn't remember leather being so supple. The last time I wore a leather jacket I was seventeen and riding a motorcycle with a boyfriend.

Do you care about color? Ethan interrupted my thoughts. 'Cause black goes with everything. That afternoon I tried on numerous black leather jackets and modeled them for my son—a new experience for both of us.

Ethan had a comment for every style I modeled for him: Big. Never! Ehh. Too plain. Are you hiding in there?

Several jackets later, he motioned to the salesperson. That's the one, he said. He reached for his billfold. It's your early Christmas gift, Mom.

Ethan was right. I wore it all the time. I still wear the jacket, and it reminds me of the times we shared together while I learned how to live on my own again.

I found an Episcopal church only four blocks from the apartment. It turned out to be the parish where my maid-of-honor's father had been the rector, which helped me feel more comfortable—at least there was a connection with my previous life. The first time I entered the church building I sat in the back, trying to be inconspicuous. I had just received notice that my divorce was final, and although I was relieved, I felt like a piece of discarded fruit left on the ground to rot. It was still a stretch for me to get through an entire church service without crying, and moving to LA hadn't changed that. I was still wrestling with the enormity of Mark's deception.

After a few Sundays, I decided to attend the adult-education class, which was held after the nine o'clock service. I knew they'd be asking thoughtful questions, even if they weren't ones I was struggling with. The rector, Father Shaw, led the group with a joyful immediacy about him that put everyone at ease. We were starting a book titled *Grace*. Two weeks into the class, we read a vignette about a married couple in which the husband was gay. The author, who was a priest, was a close friend of theirs and explained that he couldn't bring himself to tell his friend's wife that her husband was gay.

As I read that part of the book, my stomach tightened, and I was uneasy about going to the next class, but I showed up anyway. Ten of us were seated around the table. The rector began with a prayer and asked if anything had caught our attention, and we all began talking. By the end of the hour, we had touched on all the readings except the author's personal admission. We sat in uncomfortable silence.

Lies steal the truth, I said quietly. I hadn't expected to talk about my marriage, but I found myself telling them about my husband and how I learned he was gay.

I don't think there's any grace in a lie, I said. Some class members nodded their heads in agreement. Hesitantly I added: My husband was an Episcopal priest. I glanced around the table to see if anyone appeared upset by what I had revealed. A few stared down at the table. One woman covered her mouth and was slowly shaking her head.

An older gentleman seated across the table from me leaned toward me and in a gentle voice said, I was married to a lesbian for many years, but we were more fortunate than you, I think. My wife and I learned together that she was a lesbian. It was a discovery for both of us. It was different from the kind of pain you experienced. He stretched his hands out to me. I'm sorry for what's happened to you. I think in time God's grace will reveal itself to you; perhaps it will happen, as it often does, in ways you never expected.

I hope you're right. I was trembling. Thank you for being willing to tell me about that part of your life. I don't feel so alone anymore. There's grace in that. I was thankful for his honesty and relieved by his reaching out to me. It was a gift to feel seen and respected. Maybe I wasn't such damaged goods after all.

After class, the rector asked me if I'd like to meet with him to discuss what I revealed that morning in class. I accepted his offer, and for the next few weeks we met in his church office. He listened carefully as I poured out the struggle I was having, always thinking about Mark's betrayals. He asked if I was seeing a professional counselor. I told him I was. I added that I knew it was imperative for my health that I forgive myself as well as Mark, but I admitted that getting my head and heart around my emotions was more than a challenge. I don't know how to start, I said.

During one of our last talks, he said he had given much thought about the word *forgive* and asked if I could "give forth," as in letting go. Can you imagine yourself holding Mark up to God and asking God to do the forgiving?

I can try, I said as I struggled to form a picture in my mind. God, whatever you are, you'll have to do the forgiving, because I can't do that right now.

I often cringed when I practiced the image Father Shaw suggested, but as time passed, Mark seemed more of a phenomenon and less of a person, and that helped me to let go of some my anger. It would take me much longer to forgive myself.

The following week when class was finished, the man seated next to me asked me if I'd join him for coffee at the bookstore across the street. Pleasantly surprised, I agreed to go, and over the next few months, I got to know Henry. We often had coffee after church as we shared our life stories with one another. I was sorry to say good-bye to him when he left. In an e-mail six months later, he said he was engaged to marry the woman he had often spoken about and thanked me for listening to him. He said he'd learned a lot about himself during our discussions. I was pleased he valued me as a good listener.

One evening, feeling alone and bored, I looked up "straight wife" on the Internet and was surprised to find a Web page called the Straight Wives Network. I tried entering one of the chat rooms, but when I finally figured out how to access the site, I didn't feel ready to talk with strangers. Not long after that, I got an e-mail from a friend back home. She told me that after her divorce she found a dance partner online. I'd never heard of online dating and didn't think I'd feel comfortable, but being curious, I answered her e-mail with a phone call and lots of questions. Then I launched myself into a new venture: Match.com.

My first online date was with a man who, after a recent divorce, had returned to LA to live with his mother. Most of the evening, he talked about his former wife and the care he was giving his mom. A few weeks later, I exchanged e-mails with a man from Northern California who was grieving his wife's death. He told me the plans the two of them had for their grandkids, for travel, and for their future. We talked on the phone each week for a while, forming a friendship over the phone. We were both wrestling mightily with grief and found comfort in sharing conversation.

I was managing to get through day by day, but I wasn't engaged in life. I was hiding from myself, trying to escape the emptiness that hung around me like a heavy, metal cloak. It was just before Christmas when I screwed up enough courage to walk more than six blocks from my apartment. I spotted a hair salon, and there I met Leila, the shop's owner. She was blow-drying my hair when a young man—later I learned he was her son—handed her a letter. She dropped the dryer and ran to the back of the shop. The other clients sat quietly under their hairdryers as though they had seen this kind of scene before. Several minutes passed before she returned. She was hyperventilating, and her hands were shaking as she finished my hair. I don't know what to do, she said as she grasped the back of my chair. This happens to me, and I can't get my breath. I get scared.

I stood up and, turning to face her, I said, Leila, I'm a nurse. I think I can help you. You're having a panic attack. I've had lots of them. Take a breath and let it out slowly, *very* slowly. I gently touched her shoulder. Again, very slowly, let the air out. Better? She nodded.

Will you walk with me for a few minutes, just outside the shop?

I'll try, she whispered.

Good, let's try it together, breathing slowly, like I said. As we walked, I encouraged her to talk. She told me that her husband was filing for divorce and returning to Iran. She wiped away the tears. Putting my arm around her shoulder, I reminded her to take slow, deep breaths. I could feel her relax. Feeling better now?

Yes, I am! You're an angel, you know.

No, I'm not. I've just had a divorce, and I am not an angel. I was glad I could help her. We turned back toward the shop.

Her dark eyes showed surprise, but her face softened. You, divorced?

Yes, I learned my ex-husband was gay.

Oh no! That's terrible, just terrible. You and I, we need to talk. Do you want to have dinner tomorrow night with me? The shop closes at five-thirty, and we could go to one of the restaurants near here. The smell of shampoo and ammonia wafted toward us from her shop. I could meet you here. I nodded yes.

As we entered her shop, she motioned to the other clients and exclaimed, This lovely lady here, she's my guardian angel.

My friendship with Leila began that day. It was later that I realized I could turn my anxiety disorder into an asset that could help others.

On My Own

We must find within us the will to grieve and
to live at the same time.

—*Joan D. Chittister*

Christmas of the new millennium, 2000, arrived
quickly that year. I'd only been sleeping in my rental
apartment for two weeks when I realized it was the
first time in my life I didn't have a Christmas tree; even
when I was pregnant and living on my own in Berkeley,
I had purchased a tiny tree. I thought that Angela and
Ethan would mention buying a tree, but they never
did, and I didn't want to ask. They were generous to
have invited me into their lives, and I didn't want to
appear ungrateful or too demanding. I wished that I
could surprise them like Mary Poppins, show up with
a tree all trimmed with gifts around it and a table full
of goodies I'd baked. What a fantasy that was; I hardly
had the energy to drive myself to their home on Christ-

mas Day. We all sank into their large leather couch and stared at a football game. I was thankful I hadn't had an anxiety attack since arriving in LA.

I could make it to the grocery to buy food for my cats without getting too anxious, but I wasn't eating much myself. Frozen suppers tasted like stale potatoes and wax paper. I still didn't enjoy my own company enough to relax and have dinner. I drank liquid supplements to keep me going, but I was losing weight. When I looked in the mirror, I saw a pinched face and said to myself, You look like an old crone. I consumed movies, mostly Sundance and foreign films. When each video ended, I put in another. Day or night, it didn't matter.

I tried to help my body get in better shape by signing up for three months of the beginners' class at the yoga studio not far away, but my body betrayed me: when I laid on my stomach, I couldn't raise my head off the mat. When I rolled over on my back and tried to raise my legs off the floor, they trembled uncontrollably. I was so weak I couldn't hold the simplest pose for more than twenty seconds. I quit the class and tried to walk the beach again, but I felt panicky being alone for that long without being able to contact Ethan if I needed him. I took refuge in my apartment during long, purposeless days—awake until three in the morning and up again at six. Encased in my nightgown, I took up residence on the couch and went days without showering, trying to manage the unmanageable.

One day shortly after Christmas, I remembered that I still hadn't reviewed the floppy disc I found on the rug in Mark's study the day the movers came. I finally found it tucked inside the binder where I put copies of our Christmas letters, and I stuck it into the computer. It appeared to be a journal of Mark's, started in 1988, which was after we'd been told to attend the AA groups for sex addicts and codependents, and after we had seen addiction counselors.

It was filled with descriptions of what he had done, who he thought he really was, and ways he had used our children and me. There were dated entries that commented on his daily activities and emotional struggles. He often seemed to be in a dialogue with himself and with God. The diary filled well over fifty single-spaced pages. I was repulsed and horrified when I finished reading it. I didn't sleep much that night. I needed to talk to someone about what I'd read, but I didn't know who.

The next morning, I opened Mark's journal again and quickly closed it. The bishop should have the diary. No, not the bishop. When I saw the bishop six weeks earlier, I had expected he would contact Child Protective Services in Madison. If he had, CPS probably would have wanted to interview me to determine what I knew, if anything. But to date no one from CPS had contacted me. My attorney had specifically said to let the bishop handle it; however, it seemed to me that my bishop wasn't doing anything. As a licensed registered nurse, I felt I had an obligation to inform the authorities. They could take it from there.

I called CPS in California, which was where Mark told me he first had anonymous sex, in 1975. They connected me immediately to a caseworker, and I hurriedly explained that I was an RN and needed to tell someone what I had found. She asked me questions, and I told her what I knew. She said she was quite aware of situations similar to what I had described. I'll do some research, she said, but then explained that since so much time had passed since we lived in California, she wasn't certain she'd find anything. She thanked me for contacting her and told me I had done the right thing. That was nice to hear, but as I sat there afterward, I didn't think I could put behind me all that had happened.

I decided then that no matter how demanding it would be, I had to write my story. That was the way I could help others. At the time, I didn't know that writing my story would lead me down my own road to recovery.

The second week in January, I had a petrifying panic attack. I couldn't swallow, my heart was racing, I felt I was suffocating. I closed my eyes and struggled to escape myself. I called Ethan. He came over and listened to me as I talked my way through it.

As my anxiety decreased, Ethan looked at me intently, and with a slight quiver in his voice he said, You know, Mom, you had the luxury of divorcing Dad. I will take him with me to my grave.

I felt ashamed and hung my head. I had been thoughtless and self-centered. I wasn't the only one who was hurting. I'd only been married to his dad, not tied to him by common genes. I thought of Lexa. She must be hurting too. I hadn't been much help to her either.

Two days later, Ethan and Angela arrived unan-
nounced at my apartment and told me they had made
an appointment with a Dr. Solomon for the following
afternoon. Ethan listed the doctor's credentials, including the fact that he had done research in psychophar-
macology at UCLA. He knew that would reassure me
of the doctor's competence.

I went to bed early that evening and the next
morning was surprised when I realized it was the first
time I had slept through the night since arriving in
LA. I knew I needed help, but not wanting to admit
it, I made nasty faces at Angela and Ethan when they
arrived at my door that afternoon. I rode down in the
elevator with them, walked out onto the sidewalk, and
then sauntered past Ethan's Mustang. He came up
behind me and gently took my arm. Mom, don't make
a scene. Which was worse, I wondered, making a fuss
in the street where people could see me, or going to the
doctor as they had arranged? I got in the car.

Dr. Solomon turned out to be only three years older
than Ethan. He listened to my story and then appealed
to my nursing experience by emphasizing the side
effects of stress. I knew it could be a killer but thought
I'd gotten used to it, as if a body ever adjusts to chronic
stress.

I think you can probably gut out this depression.
His voice was gentle and reassuring. I don't have any
doubt that you have the emotional strength to do that.
What I worry about is the toll this stress will take
on you. He folded his hands on his desk and leaned
forward.

I know what you're saying, I said. I just hate the thought of taking meds. They mess with my head. I felt calmer but trapped.

What if we started you out on the very smallest dose? It's now available in a liquid. You could start with two and a half milligrams and build up over the next several weeks, eventually to ten milligrams. See how it affects you. Some people, perhaps like you who are very sensitive to meds, can tell in just a few days if they feel better. He looked at me for a response.

I'm thinking about it, I said, looking down at the floor.

Gale—may I call you that?

I nodded yes.

Well then, Gale, I know this isn't the same thing, but I was engaged for six years to the love of my life. And then, just days before we were to be married, she told me she was a lesbian.

That must have been a terrible shock. I'm sorry to hear that. I leaned back in my chair for a moment and thought about the man at church, with the lesbian wife. I really wasn't the only one after all. There were others who had suffered the loss of a lover or a spouse in the same way. In my ignorance, I had assumed I was a solo act. In the years that followed, of course, I learned that many marriages were disrupted because one of the members was not clear about or had hidden his or her sexual preference.

Yes, mind-blowing, he said. I don't think it compares with the thirty-five years you had, but I do know something about that kind of pain.

It wipes you off the face of the earth. It's a complete dismissal of you as a sexual human being, I said.

That's right. He paused. The medication, I think, will help to take the edge off. You can always discontinue it if you want.

I thought for a few minutes. I'd been running scared for so long; at least the meds could be regulated; I didn't want to be plowed under like I was when prescribed Thorazine as a teenager. I agreed to try it.

Dr. Solomon explained that I'd had a reactive depression and cautioned me that it would take time to work through it. He made an appointment for me two weeks out, adding that he was available by pager twenty-four hours a day, and he asked me to check in with him in ten days—or sooner if I wished. You're seeing someone here that you can talk with?

Yes, I have a counselor. She was recommended to me before I left home. She mostly just listens to me.

Having someone listen to you is very important.

Okay, then—the meds and the talking. I'm certain my son and daughter-in-law will be relieved.

You have a wonderful son and a very concerned daughter-in-law, he said, handing me the prescription and walking with me to the waiting room.

I took my first dose the next morning, thinking of my friend Ruthie. She had died several years before my divorce. I missed our weekly lunches together, her friendship, and her astute advice. Hey you, I said aloud. You always said there was no point in making everything harder on ourselves. So here goes. I filled the small plastic syringe with the gooey clear liquid, and lifting it skyward, said, I'm taking this 'cause you did. You were so brave. I'm trying to be brave too. You and I could have had some tears and laughs over this one.

The thick, bitter fluid burned my tongue. I washed it down with lots of water, wondering how long it would take to work. Hugging myself, I thought, I am going to get through this. My kids expect that from me and so would Ruthie.

Within the week, I already felt less scattered and anxious, and I could think more clearly. Ethan and Angela also suggested that we eat together every Wednesday evening. I think they wanted to see if my medication was working. They'd provide dessert; my job was to bring dinner. That meant going to the grocery routinely and staying longer than was comfortable—in other words, I *had* to control my anxiety or no dinner with the kids.

I knew my fears were irrational, but I didn't want people seeing me struggling for air and looking weird. I didn't want anyone judging me. My ever-present inner critic claimed that respectable people didn't make a commotion. It took me several weeks to desensitize myself. I pictured abandoned grocery carts, full of colorful fruits and vegetables, sitting in the middle of the aisles and decided that "carts without shoppers" was what happened when someone had an anxiety attack or had to leave. I called it the "anxious shopper exit." I tried out my theory, leaving my cart full and walking out the door empty-handed. Nothing happened. No one came after me. The store was still there the next time I shopped. From then on, I gave myself permission to leave my cart if I had to, confident that I wouldn't cause a crisis. Now whenever I see a ditched cart, I smile to myself, realizing that from time to time we all need to exit and regroup.

Late one afternoon in early February, I decided to phone Madeline, the one other person I knew in LA. Over the years we had kept in touch, but we hadn't seen each other since we were teenagers. I recognized her laughter. You must come over. Bring the kiddies, Angela and Ethan. I want to meet them soon.

She was standing in her doorway as we climbed out of the car. Come here, darlings. I need to hug you all. She opened her arms as her face blossomed into the beautiful smile that I hadn't forgotten. Her auburn hair brushed my cheek as she gave me a kiss. She stood back, studying the three of us. Well, we finally got you to Hollywood! You look great. Come in, all of you, please. Follow me, she said, looking over her shoulder. I hope you didn't have much dinner. Somehow, we always start with dessert. She laughed as she pointed to an array of goodies on the dining-room table. Please help yourselves and get comfy she said, looking at Angela and Ethan. Hubby will be here in a second. He loves to have company when he's reviewing the Oscar nominees. Your mom and I are going to the library to have a chat.

Having Madeline sweep me into her arms and her life was a better tonic than Prozac. We enjoyed revisiting our past: the desperately earnest teenage talks, the silly pranks we pulled to annoy our house mother, and the songs we sang for the laundry driver who made his delivery in the predawn hours. Madeline grinned. Do you remember the night we planned to run away from school? We were dressed in our PJs and had just raided the kitchen for peach ice cream, my favorite.

I know. I wanted caramel, but there wasn't any. We snuck back upstairs and scrambled out onto the roof. Wasn't it early fall? Still warm out? We could barely see the lights across the Hudson River.

She asked me to tell her my story, what had happened over all those years. She wanted to hear everything.

Oh, Madeline, you don't need to hear all that; it's just a mess. I mean I'm a mess.

You don't look a mess to me—tired maybe. Too thin, yes. But not a mess. She reached out and touched my shoulder.

You're kind.

I'm honest. It's going to take you a while to heal, my dear.

Oh, I know that. It's like Fritz Perls said, "You can't push the river; it flows by itself." I just hope it won't go on forever.

It won't, but it'll seem like it at times. I want you to know I'm here. You can call me anytime. If you want me to listen, I will. If you want to scream, that's fine by me. You want to walk and talk, or walk and no talk, either way.

I looked down at my hand at the space where my wedding band used to be and said, Do you remember reading *The Scarlet Letter* in English class?

Of course! Poor Hester Prynne, and it wasn't really her fault.

Well, that's what I feel like. I think everyone must be staring at me, whispering, pointing behind my back saying, "She's the one. Her husband lied. He was gay and didn't tell her, poor thing. How stupid not to know."

You couldn't have known. That's the point. You've told me not even the shrinks you saw knew, or if they did, they didn't tell you. Mark was a skilled actor. It wasn't your fault.

I can't be a man for him, that's for sure.

And you don't want to be! Come here. She patted the couch beside her. You've always been strong, you've always believed in yourself, you've always stood up for what was right, and that's what you're going to do again.

I don't think I ever told her how important her friendship was to me. During that spring of 2001, as Madeline and I reminisced, I began to catch glimpses of the younger me: my energy, my sense of humor, and my boundless delight in the world around me. Being with her reminded me who I was before Mark. The woman I was then had checked out years ago, probably not long after I was married.

Gradually I began to bring order to my days. The medicine helped, and my outlook on life began to shift. I began by doing nice things for myself. I bought fragrant flowers—spring daffodils and tuber rose—tried on new clothes, and changed my hairstyle. I had my nails manicured. I was cautious, but I no longer felt the need to hide.

Leila, my hairdresser and new friend, and I went out

to dinner together regularly. One evening she invited me to her home. Her daughter's family was visiting, and I asked to hold her new grandson. I wondered as I looked at him if I would ever hold a grandchild of my own.

Before I left that evening, she whispered to me, You need to loosen up a little. Why don't you treat yourself to a massage? I could think of lots of reasons why not, but she saw me scowl and said, I know just the person, two blocks up and one over. She has her own studio. I've been to her myself. Go! So I made an appointment.

I lay on the unfamiliar table naked except for my briefs. The sheets were warm and smooth. The background music was a nature track: waves breaking on the ocean shore, humpback whales calling to one another. My body slid into softness. I closed my eyes and watched the bright begonia colors of my grandmother's summer garden dance on the back of my eyelids. The therapist came quietly into the room, her firm, confident hands moving deftly across my back. Silently my eyes filled with tears as she worked on my tired tenseness. Not only had my body been affected by the years with Mark, but my mind and spirit had suffered as well. The massage helped me to settle into a more peaceful way with myself, something I needed to practice every day.

The citrus trees were beginning to bloom when, in a burst of unusual enthusiasm, I phoned several organizations until I found a weekend workshop for writers. I signed up immediately and asked Ethan if he'd go to

UCLA with me. I didn't know where the campus was, and I still didn't like driving very far from my apartment. Of course, he answered. I'll even take notes.

The first question the professor asked was how many of us had business cards. A third of the class put up a hand. You can't call yourself a writer if you don't have a card to pass out, said the prof. That's the first thing you need to do. The next day I went out and ordered my cards.

I did my best to write every day, trying to make sense of my life, telling my story to the stuffed toy monkey who hung by his arm from the lamp near my desk. The words I wrote held painful memories. But I continued writing because I had to reclaim my own heart and soul. I wrote about what happened, what I missed, and what I avoided. It was like creating a ledger sheet: counting up, listing, going over, and recounting repeatedly, as if by some miracle I could change the past. Soon I discovered that I needed more options. I ditched my yellow legal pad and placed my Mac on the desktop. With an energy that surprised me, I swiftly typed whole paragraphs.

When I completed my story—several years and eight hundred pages later—I realized that I was writing myself into healing. It had taken me a long time to recognize we were both so strangled by denial that we couldn't have shared our fears with one another. Then I remembered hearing something Nelson Mandela had said, that without the truth there could not be any reconciliation.

Cleaning House

> Understanding does not cure evil, but it is a
> definite help inasmuch as one can cope with
> a comprehensible darkness.
>
> —*Carl Jung*

During the early spring of 2001, I tried to adjust to the little part of Los Angeles where I lived, Santa Monica, but it wasn't the Mediterranean mecca I had expected. It did have a glorious beachfront, if not examined too closely. I hoped to walk in the park after my disappointment with the beach, but during the day, it was overflowing with homeless folks pushing their grocery carts aimlessly from one dead end to another. In the evenings, I saw them curled up in doorways, sleeping on pieces of cardboard. Adding their misery to my own, I was still hauling a backpack of sorrow around with me much of the time, so the park was not an inviting place either.

The apartment beneath mine was being renovated. The constant jackhammering was so jarring that if there had been an earthquake, I wouldn't have felt it, and it didn't help my anxiety either. Along with all the noise, blackouts were pulsing through the city that spring. They had something to do with PGE and illegal shutdowns of the electrical grid. Just the thought of getting caught in my apartment elevator during a blackout unnerved me enough to keep me in at times.

Under Dr. Solomon's direction, I slowly increased the dose of the antidepressant medication. Although I hadn't yet reached the level he prescribed, I was feeling strong enough to return to Madison. It was time to pack up the house Mark and I had designed, move out, and begin to make new memories.

A late-March snowfall covered the still-cold ground. Not even Lenten rose or blue Scylla were pushing through the snow as I walked into our old home. The air inside reminded me of a mausoleum, damp and musty. Packing up would be a chore, but the naïve, desperate, and dependent-on-Mark part of me had changed. In California, I had taken several steps on the road to living again. I didn't know how long my journey would be, but now I was determined to succeed.

I had been back in Madison only a few days when my friend Kris phoned, reminding me that we needed to walk every afternoon. When she first saw me, she frowned. You look gaunt and skinny. You need to eat more.

At least I'm alive, and I *am* better than a year ago.

You're right; you are. With a smile, she scanned me up and down and pointed at my skinny legs. However, a little more muscle there would be nice.

They've always been that way, I insisted. Skinny legs run in my family, I said a bit defensively.

Yada, yada. It's time to buy a bike; then you can change that a bit. She started running in place. Aerobics would be good for you too. She looked like sunshine as she bounced in front of me, her blond curls bobbing. We walked together for more than an hour, teasing and laughing with one another as though nothing awful had ever happened.

That evening I decided to tackle the music library that Mark and I had collected over the years. I couldn't have predicted that holding a CD in my hand would remind me of so many details of our life together. I stacked the discs by composer and artist and noticed that there were multiples of the same symphony and concerto—not even different musicians, but *identical* recordings. Was this duplication a result of Mark's lying? Did he stop by stores to buy something for an alibi, trying to cover the fact he had been cruising for sex?

When I finished the CDs, I started to go through the LPs. Some of them had belonged to our parents. They only filled two boxes: his and hers. What I really dreaded was going through the old cassettes. It took an hour to match them with their plastic cases. I came across a few that had no labels, undoubtedly ones that Mark had made some years earlier. I popped one in an old boom box and pressed the play button. I heard a man's voice talking deliberately and slowly, but I didn't recognize who the speaker was. Seconds passed before I realized I was listening to Mark as he dictated his students' quarterly report cards. But what I heard wasn't his usual voice. His words sounded as though they had been put through a sieve, pinched and higher in register than was his normal range. Suddenly I caught a cadence that startled me. His speech reminded me of the gay men I knew. Now I understood that was Mark's *real* voice, the one he had concealed throughout our married years. I was puzzled why he had left the tape there. It wasn't like him to forget things.

After the music was divided and boxed up, I was ready to label the photo albums for Lexa and Ethan. As I flipped through our pictures, I realized I would hold the memory of our broken family in my heart for years. But would they want to be reminded of these fragments of our family?

Early the next morning, Emily, with whose family I had gratefully spent the previous Thanksgiving, called and asked if she could come for a visit. She bounced in, looking tanned, with her unruly hair tied back in a crimson scarf and said, Are you ready for the closet attack? It's time for a new wardrobe. I hear your clothes are too big and you need updating.

We went immediately to my closet. Without pausing, she set up the rules. Three piles, she said: out, keep, and maybe—no going back once you've made a decision.

You're tough. Do you do this a lot?

She grinned. Believe me, yes. With twin girls, it's a

must. I have lots of experience. Trust me. Emily started at one side of the closet. Holding each garment next to me, she checked to see if the color and style were flattering. Searching my face for clues, she said, Yes, no, or maybe?

Emily turned the afternoon into Comedy Central as she commented on my clothing. This must have looked great in the Sixties, she said, holding up my denim bell-bottoms. Wait, here's a real treat, something from high school perhaps? Ahh, and this must be your grand-mother's nightdress? We were both laughing.

When the closet was almost empty, Emily said, Okay! That's good work. But before I leave, two important areas: shoes and nightgowns. Gotta go through both of those before we quit or we haven't done our job. A lot of shoes went out that day. Emily grinned. Just think what Imelda Marcos had to tackle. Now then, the nightgowns. Out. All of them.

All of them? I felt a little guilty—I knew I should have gotten rid of them earlier.

That's the best thing to do, unless you can give me a good reason to keep them. And of course, there's the underwear....

I went to Victoria's Secret when I was out in LA, I said in a hurry, pleased that I'd at least done part of the sorting out.

Terrific! You see—it wasn't that bad. She reached for the purse she'd hung on the door handle.

Well, not really. I guess beginnings hide in endings. The trick is to find where. I felt relieved but also vulnerable. Part of my identity was going out the door with my clothes, and I didn't have anything to replace it.

Later that evening I tackled one more chore: my jewelry box. I saved it for last because it was the most difficult—tied to sentiments, specific events, and monetary value. The thought of wearing any jewelry that Mark had given me made me cringe. I didn't want anything around me that he'd touched. Of course, that was impossible.

I had already cut my wedding ring in half and buried it unceremoniously in the backyard—following an idea I picked up that anything blessed should be either buried or burned. Then there was my engagement ring, which Mark had helped design. He had apologized when he put it on my finger, claiming one of the three emeralds was imperfect. I held my hand up to the sun and stared at the dazzling green stones channel-set in a narrow gold band but couldn't spot the flaw. He had to show it to me. I added the ring to the "out" pile.

Picking up my beautiful gold and sapphire bracelet, I thought about the day in Elmwood Heights when Mark and I were window-shopping downtown. He surprised me with the bracelet on Christmas of 1968. He shouldn't have spent the money his grandmother had given him for medical school, but secretly I was pleased he did. I had dreamed about the dainty gold band with its tiny blue stones, but now holding it in my hands made me feel I'd been greedy. I found several other pieces in the box, including my yellow jade necklace, that looked dreadful on me. Mark had exceptional taste. However, like my mother, he gave me elegant gifts that were often the wrong color or size—which always made me feel that neither of them saw the real me. Finally, I opened a small black velvet box revealing a single cabochon emerald, his gift to me on our last anniversary, a time of conflict and bitterness. I wasn't certain if I wanted to give it back to him or keep it.

After a restless night, I decided to get rid of all the pieces he'd given me. Feeling embarrassed about selling jewelry, I quickly handed the jeweler my tainted bundle. I wondered what he thought as he peered through his loupe at each item. Did he think my family was going through hard times? We were, of course, but not the kind he might have imagined. I felt sleazy and hoped no one I knew would walk in. After I ditched the jewelry, I had the house painted a cheerful yellow—a final attempt to cover the past. Then I put it on the market.

During that first summer after my divorce, I returned to Joan, the psychiatrist who had counseled me right after Mark left. During our sessions, I often felt like a tornado had swept through my life, leaving pieces of me jumbled and strewn around. I couldn't find a place to be safe—where I could stop moving, where I could be still and think. I had lived in tandem with Mark for so many years I had forgotten who I was or who I used to be.

How could he have done that to me, I repeatedly asked my psychiatrist. I don't understand how anyone could do that.

During a session one day that summer, I asked her again, How could...She gave me a gentle smile and said, Gale, if you did understand, I'd be worried about you.

I never asked that question again, although I continued seeing her for several years.

It took me a long time to accept the fact that during our marriage I tolerated Mark's emotional distance because I believed that simply his presence helped me cope with my anxiety.

Joan continually reminded me that I was emotionally wiser now. Remember, be as kind to yourself as you are to others, she said.

I would need to hold onto that and apply it in the years to come.

ʕ

Now that my home was on the market, I needed to find another place to live. I was really looking for a brand-new life, but that wasn't going to happen anytime soon. I settled for an uninspired two-bedroom bungalow in a nearby community where all the houses had red geraniums in their window boxes. Geraniums made me sneeze, so I planted white daisies and larkspur-blue hydrangeas outside my front door. I made a few changes in the house, carefully choosing new paint and wallpaper. The modifications I made in my new house paralleled the adjustments I was trying to make in my life. Undertaking a project was one of the easiest ways for me to escape the ache that still stalked me.

Another way I tried to avoid the painful present was to travel back in time to the summers when I was a little girl. I had spent weeks with Edith's family—my second family, as I referred to them—on their farm. I remembered when Edith's older brother, Uncle Karl, had given me my first job: gathering the eggs. He showed me how to open the screen door to the hen house quietly, so as not to disturb the chickens. Slowly I slipped my hand under the downy breast of the first hen. It was warm and soft. Not wanting to scare her, I waited a few moments before wrapping my fingers around the egg. Then I moved back, step by step, staring at the perfect white orb I held in my hand. I always respected the proud white ladies sitting on their gold straw thrones. I never once got pecked.

Coming out of my reverie, I lectured myself: You have got to get out of this house.

You are still hiding! A few days later, I returned to a nearby art center, this time as a student. Years ago, when living in California, I had learned how to center clay on a kick wheel, but now, since I wasn't feeling focused yet myself, I thought I'd try bronze casting instead. It sounded bold and demanding, and I thought it might be a good stretch for me artistically and emotionally.

The teacher said to make something in clay first, so I grabbed a handful and began rolling it out flat like cookie dough. Delighted to feel as though I were in kindergarten again, I cut out nine narrow pieces each about six inches long and a quarter-inch wide. They were slats for a park bench like the ones at the zoo where I played as a three-year-old. Then I tried making a street lamp, the old-fashion kind with kerosene lanterns at the top. It looked like the lamps that lined the narrow sidewalks where my grandparents had their summer home. I had spent many summers there with them as a young girl.

I was trying to create a small art installation in bronze, and I wasn't certain how it would look when I was finished. I put the street lamp next to the little bench. On the other side of the bench, I placed a smooth, speckled rock that I found one summer on a sandy beach. As I played with the clay, it began to take the form of a naked woman. She was nine inches long, and I shaped her body so that she could sit on the bench. Her arms were crossed; her tiny feet were firmly on the ground. But she didn't have a head yet.

I was stumped. I had no idea how to sculpt a clay head. Frustrated, I pinched a piece of clay from her back and began to warm it in my hands. Back and forth, I caressed it until I was surprised to see it curve; it resembled a bird feather. I snatched more clay and made other feathers like the first until there were several rippling structures sweeping upward from her shoulders. They were radiant after she was cast in bronze. I placed her under the streetlight, relaxing on a park bench. The sculpture glowed as if on fire. She was me, and I liked her very much.

My lady was not a masterpiece, but I remembered a sign on the front lawn of a small New England church Mark and I passed when we drove Lexa to college in 1995. It announced the title of the Sunday service:

"Loss Makes Artists of Us All." I wondered who else in my class might be casting their story in bronze.

ભ્

The silvery green sumac were beginning to show their ginger-colored underskirts, hinting that fall would come sooner than I thought, and I began to feel apprehensive. I had settled into my new home and promptly had a garage sale. I sold most of the things Mark and I had bought together, even furniture. I was trying to start over, and I didn't want to hang around old memories. I wanted to fall in love with life again. But how? I knew I didn't want to spend the winter in Madison. It would be cold and dreary, and after being in Santa Monica for the previous winter, I knew I liked the sunshine, but I couldn't go back there and make myself a nuisance for Angela and Ethan. I had to make my own life now.

One particularly beautiful day in late August, I went outside to get a few zinnias from my tiny backyard garden, and instead I sat down in the old rocker from my mother's laundry room. I closed my eyes and felt the late-summer sun on my face. For a moment I thought about the Arizona sun and how we'd vacationed there with the kids, and then, pushing Mark out of my mind, I remembered another Arizona and the times I'd spent in Tucson as a young girl, visiting my grandparents in the spring, when the orange trees were in bloom and their sweet citrus perfume hovered in the cool night air.

I swayed back and forth faster now in the rocker, thinking about what Mom had said to me in 1959, shortly after my birth-daughter was born. Mother had spoken to me on the phone. You need to be in Tucson for Easter with your grandparents, she said. And don't you dare say anything about was has happened. They'd just die if they knew. I signed you up for a weight-loss program in Berkeley. You need to attend twice a week. Lose twenty pounds before you join your grandparents. I followed all her instructions.

Oblivious to my postpartum condition, my grandparents treated me as they always had, with unconditional love. Although I felt fragile and empty, I knew that my mother expected me to carry on, so I deep-sixed my feelings. I swam early in the morning before many guests were at the pool, and in the late afternoon, I played tennis, which helped me to retrieve my figure quickly. Thinking back, I realized that exercising so much during those two weeks probably squelched any postpartum depression I might have had.

☙

Suddenly I felt cold. The sun had dropped behind the roof of my house. I opened my eyes. I knew what I had to do now. I would go to Arizona for the winter. After all, I still had the house in Tucson, the one Mark and I were going to retire to someday. I'd have to find another place to live there, but I'd just done that and I could do it again.

I drove south to Tucson shortly after the shocking 9/11 terrorist attacks. My personal grief was superseded by the bigger disasters at the World Trade Center and the Pentagon. The desert sun seemed subdued by the senseless loss of life—but I was alive and, although feeling cautious, still eager to move ahead.

Once again, I started the process of settling in. This time was easier because I had asked Ethan, Angela, and Lexa to join me for Thanksgiving. I planned to critique some houses before they arrived. Then they could help me decide which one was the best choice. We would decide together, and I would make my memories with them now.

ᘓ

One afternoon early in October, I returned to the little mission church I had visited forty-two years before, when I was twenty. It was 1959, and I left the Bay Area to attend summer session at the University of Arizona before reentering UC Berkeley in the fall.

The moment I looked down the church aisle to the arched window behind the altar, I was swept back in time. The sparsely vegetated mountains looked the same, but now a large eucalyptus tree almost hid their broken profile. I came to this church that summer after my father phoned me with the terrible news that Grant, my first love, had committed suicide. I had seen him only a few weeks earlier and told him I would catch up with him in the fall when I returned to Berkeley. At the time, there were signs: Grant was acting odd and brought a handgun into my apartment. I didn't like it, but I didn't know what to do about it either. The morning I left for Arizona, he pleaded with me not to go, but I had my plans. I blew him a kiss as I stepped into my car.

A few days into classes, my dad phoned. I screamed as he told me Grant was dead. I know, I said. I had a dream about him last night—there was blood everywhere outside the second-story window where the fire escape is. I felt suspended in nowhere, frightened and overwhelmed.

Maybe Grant wouldn't have taken his life that summer if I had stayed. I'll always wonder. I blamed myself, of course. Not completely, but enough to carry him with me for the rest of my life.

Now, back in Tucson once more, I needed to find the energy and guts to heal. I pulled the kneeler out from under the pew, knelt down, and begged God for help. Years ago, the quiet spaciousness of the desert had helped me mend. I hoped it could restore me again.

Learning to Heal

Grief is about a broken heart, not a broken
brain.

—*Russell & Friedman, Grief Recovery*

Ethan, Angela, and Lexa came to Tucson for Thanksgiving weekend, and I was elated to be with them
again. We found a house that all of us thought I should
buy. To celebrate, we danced around in my new dining
room just before I signed the purchase agreement.

After the New Year's holidays, in January of 2002,
my energy returned, and momentarily I scurried
around town buying things to decorate my new home.
But within the week, I withdrew again and spent my
days at the kitchen table studying the desert mountains
and the endless sky, watching as the Gambel's quail
and Cooper's hawks staked out their territories in
my backyard desert. I had sold Mark's and my home,
moved twice, settled, and resettled, and clearly none of

those efforts seemed to dismiss my continued dissatisfaction with the diocesan bishop in Madison.

I thought back to April of the previous year, when I had received a letter from the bishop. I had done exactly what he had asked when we first met: looked over the notes he had taken during our meeting and made some suggestions. Of course I remembered what Mark revealed in his document: his arrest in a department-store men's room, and his twelve hundred visits to hot johns. I had begun to comprehend how he hid behind my anxiety as an excuse to be angry and to justify acting out. He had also written that while in college he had wondered if he might be homosexual. I tried to imagine what would have transpired between us if he had told me he was gay.

I returned the bishop's e-mail with some corrections, affirming that I wanted the Episcopal equivalent of an annulment in the Roman Church. Due to the length and breadth of Mark's abhorrent behavior, I also suggested that he be deposed.

In his letter that spring, however, the bishop confirmed that there would be no annulment or its equivalent. He added that Mark would be suspended from holy orders for at least two years, after which time his suspension would be reviewed. He advised me that the official notice of Mark's suspension would be sent out in June to several groups within the Episcopal Church. Later, the report of Mark's suspension appeared on the Internet in an Episcopal database and was available if anyone wanted to search for it.

In his final paragraph, the bishop once again suggested I seek counsel from a priest who was well trained and had gifts for spiritual healing, and added that since I had lived with this tension for so many years, my healing would likely take time. I had known it would take time, and I was already in counseling. Wait a minute, *sir*, was what I wanted to tell him. My husband has spent a lot of his married life in public places having sex with men. The least I deserve is an annulment. But I didn't dare do that.

I left the bishop's letter on my kitchen table. He didn't seem to understand. My church had failed me, just as Mark had. It took me a few days to work through my fury. Then I sat down and wrote a scathing reply to the bishop, which I didn't send.

ॐ

It was hard to believe that almost a year had passed since I had received that callous letter. I was still struggling with the bishop, and I wouldn't be satisfied until I got the annulment. But now I had a seasoned lawyer, Melissa Carr, to assist me. She was reassuring but thought it would take some time to obtain what I wanted.

Meanwhile, I continued to write my story and sometimes attended the nearby Episcopal church. I felt more like an onlooker than a participant. I didn't know if I really belonged there, but I didn't feel I had any other place of worship. I wasn't a Christian Scientist, which was what my mother had taught me when I was a little girl. I had joined the Episcopal Church as a young woman, when I was twenty-four. It was

Bishop Pike's sermons that drew me to Grace Cathedral in San Francisco. But now I didn't know what I really believed. The Nicene Creed wasn't at the center of my faith. It was what people did that mattered to me. Rabbi Hillel has been quoted as saying something that felt right to me: "What is hateful to yourself, do not do to your fellow man. That is the whole Torah; the rest is just commentary. Go and study it." But then what should I do about the Trinity? I decided to let that percolate for a while.

One Sunday at church, I learned that a program called Quest was being offered on Monday evenings. It was an opportunity to explore and share one's spiritual journey. I didn't know if I was ready for that, but I told myself I needed to try. I signed up and met some lively, kind, and encouraging people. As I listened to them talk about their spiritual journeys, I noticed that I wasn't the only one who had had a run-in with God. During each weekly assignment, I examined my religion and realized I was willing to question my own beliefs as well as the church's doctrines.

Following one of our weekly meetings, a woman in my group told me about an after-school program for young children from the nearby Pascua Yaqui reservation. Would I like to assist kids who were having trouble learning to read? I eagerly agreed. It would be only the second time since my divorce that I had reached outside myself to commit to someone else. After fourteen months, I was still raw, but so were the kids. So perhaps we would be a good fit.

The next week, I went to the Sunday-school room

and was assigned to assist an eight-year-old boy. He wiggled like a caged squirrel as I encouraged him to follow my finger and pronounce the words. Suddenly, he got up from his chair, threw down his book, and stomped on my purse on his way to the water fountain. I glanced around the room. None of the other adults had seen what happened. When he finally came back to his seat, I whispered to him, How about I read you a story instead? He nodded, and we sat down beside each other. As I began to read the story, he snuggled up beside me just a little bit and then looked up at me with tired brown eyes. In them, I could see a small person trying to make his way in a big, unknown world. I knew how he felt. We got along famously after that. I was thankful to be of some use. For the rest of the school year, I looked forward to my Wednesday afternoons and the boy who taught me about courage.

Early in February, on one of those afternoons, I paused to check the church bulletin board. The words *Grief Recovery* caught my eye. It was a counseling program to assist people who were suffering a loss. That's me, I thought, and signed up, along with five other women. Together we spent the next three months meeting weekly, learning how to recover from the emotional pain caused by loss. Like many others, I knew how to talk about grief and loss, but I didn't know how to mend. During one assignment, we had to list all the losses in our lives. The counselor encouraged us to be complete and specific. It was a distressing exercise. Along with naming the event, we had write out what we had wanted to say or do at the time but didn't. I felt I was straddling my life, one foot in the past and another in the present. I wished I could erase past events.

Certainly, the most brutal loss occurred when my father beat me. I was about ten at the time. He took me to the basement and used a piece of kindling. He motioned to me to pull down my panties. I felt the sharp edges of the wood biting my skin. When I tried to move, he whacked me harder. He stopped after a while, and I slid off his knees onto the floor. He threw the stick across the floor as he marched upstairs. The pain radiated throughout me as I walked gingerly through the basement and up the back stairs to my room.

A few days later, I snuck into my parents' bathroom to peer at my backside in their door-sized mirror. It was covered with blotchy red and purple marks. I carefully ran my fingertips over my bottom. I could feel the hot, hard welts the size of silver dollars. Scabs had formed where the kindling had cut my skin. I stared at my sores, and as I started to pull up my pants, the door burst opened. There you are! I've been looking all over for you, said my mother.

I pointed to the colors on my bottom. It really hurts, Mom.

You shouldn't be hiding in bathrooms. She began to fuss with her hair. Then, turning abruptly, she marched off. I could hear the *click, click, click* of her high heels as she pranced down the front staircase. During the next several days in classes, I had to lean far to one side or the other to avoid sitting on my sores. I didn't tell anyone, and I never completely trusted my dad again.

Years later, after my father had died and my mother's life was almost over, I talked to the woman who had been my pediatrician. I asked her what I'd been like as a kid, if I was a problem; had I done something terrible that I couldn't remember?

There was nothing wrong with you, Gale. It was your parents. Your mother was jealous of you, and your dad never seemed able to stand up to her. He never liked confrontation.

It took a long time before I realized how angry Dad must have been with my mother that day. It was Christmas, and she ordered him to ask me why I read my books, my gifts, so quickly. I was a fast reader, but I think Mom believed I was skimming the pages and thus didn't appreciate my gifts. When she questioned me, I sassed her. She retaliated by demanding that I be spanked. That was the only time my father ever hit me. I was a determined little girl, but I didn't often misbehave and have to be sent to my room.

It wasn't until I started my grief-recovery work that I saw the repeating pattern of abandonment in my life. I felt I was on an emotional roller coaster as I relived the losses in my life: my mother's love when I was a child, placing Deborah up for adoption, Grant's suicide, and the disintegration of my marriage and my family. Frequently I had an "aha" moment as I worked through the written assignments and allowed myself to experience the feelings that I had rejected and shelved at the time of the event.

As I chiseled away at my grief, I learned the grieving process had to be fully embraced—not hurried, not denied—or it would return again, more insistent than before. In order to integrate and validate myself, I needed others to hear and acknowledge my story. Then I had to learn to let go of the hurt and make space in my life for feelings other than bitterness and anxiety. I got off my merry-go-round of busyness and began to practice being instead of doing all the time.

Because I was finding a new life now, I began interacting with people on a regular basis again, which brought a sense of balance and normality into my life. Early one evening, after a drive to the mountains, I sat down alone at my kitchen table and ate the first dinner I had cooked for myself in over a year. Looking toward the radiant western sky, I watched the sun exploding through the clouds. This time it was the clouds that burst, not me. At last, I was learning to let go of the anger that had been a driving factor in my life.

I began to think of my desert home as the place where I enjoyed spending time instead of the fortress I erected to keep out my sorrows. I claimed the small yard next to my house and made vegetables grow in the rocky earth. I nested in my kitchen. I had some dark moments when I felt restricted, not quite able to spread my wings, until one day Nancy, a friend from church, said, You know that you live in your kitchen except when you sleep at night, don't you?

She was right. I had set up my computer on the kitchen table, with the phone nearby. My boom box was on the counter, with a small-screen TV next to it. I was hanging out in my kitchen like an animal in its safe hole. It was clear to me that I was often ambivalent about my ability to recover, to go it alone.

After Nancy left, I moved my computer to the extra bedroom and set up a writing area, complete with my small desk and bookcases. The following week, I added yoga classes to my activities. The first time I lay down on my back with my feet flat on the floor, my legs began to tremble, just like before.

Noticing that I was having trouble, the yoga teacher walked over to me, leaned down, and spoke softly as she put her hands on my knees. Don't worry. It's not unusual. We'll talk after class.

I feel so vulnerable, I said.

I know. It happens to us a lot. We can talk about it later if you'd like. It's common. You'll get stronger, and I promise you, the shaking will stop.

The weeks passed, and I continued to exercise. Eventually I shared my story with her. She gave me a hug and looked at me as if she'd already heard it. Three months passed before I could get through a class without my legs wobbling. I continued attending yoga classes for the next eight years, and even my sphinx pose improved. My muscles strengthened, and I began to eat more regularly.

My counselor suggested that I attend an Al-Anon group, saying that having lived with Mark, an admitted addict, I might learn how his behavior had impacted me. Acting on her suggestion, I found a Wednesday-morning group where fifteen lively, attractive women welcomed me. I listened to these women discuss their lives, their challenges, their failures, and their feelings.

Two months went by before I felt brave enough to share what had brought me there. Everyone gave me her full attention and reminded me that it would take time to heal. Over the next four years, the group listened patiently as I explained what had happened in my past and my concerns for the future. Eventually I shared that I wanted to start dating but didn't know if I was ready.

Almost two years had passed since I last tried to date. Cautiously, I approached Match.com again. I felt I was placing myself on an auction block, waiting for someone to bid for me. I still had misgivings, but I continued checking my e-mail. I had coffee dates with a number of men. One brought me a single red rose. He lived with his cat in a cabin in the New Mexico mountains. Another wanted to dance. His footwork was good, but he rarely spoke.

Then one evening I met a man who had grown up not far from where I lived as a girl. We had long conversations on the phone. He was a scientist and enjoyed classical music and jazz. He was divorced and had children almost the same age as mine. The first night he took me to dinner, I ignored the red flag as he ordered two dry martinis on the rocks. I wanted to convince myself there were good vibes between us. And so—in spite of the fact that I had worked hard to heal myself from my marriage to a man who was an admitted addict—I began a relationship with a high-functioning alcoholic. I didn't acknowledge that detail at the time. As I watched his gin bottles come and go from my home, however, I had to accept the fact that, just like with Mark, I once again tolerated emotional absence because I was afraid to be alone.

With the help of both my counselor and my Al-Anon group, I probed into my childhood. I began to appreciate how my developing a healthy sense of self-worth had been seriously challenged when I was a young girl. Then I had to examine how I got involved with people who deserted me. It was hard to admit, but I realized I needed to make some serious changes.

While in the second year of attending my Al-Anon meetings, one of the members asked if I would like to join a writers' group. She was a published writer, and I was pleased to be asked. We met two evenings a month to read and discuss our work. Several weeks went by before I got the nerve to read the first six pages of my memoir. My throat was dry, and I felt sweaty in spite of the air conditioning. As I finished reading aloud, I slowly looked up. No one left; no one looked away. They went around the table, each making helpful suggestions about clarity and phrasing. No one shamed me. In fact, they were eager to hear the next chapter. Relieved that I was accepted and my truths had been heard, I could feel my self-esteem growing. Twice a month for three years, I continued to write and listen to their feedback. My five writer friends helped me write myself into clarity and wholeness. They were my first compassionate witnesses.

During the next two years, I attended various writing classes. Some focused on the business aspects of writing, such as how to write a proposal or the query letter every agent wants. Others emphasized how to access the creative muse and provided exercises on polishing one's voice. It was a time of intellectual growth for me, almost like learning a new language. I began to focus more on how to show my pain on paper rather than to experience it repeatedly. Once my story was on paper, the past became more manageable. Now as I wrote, the words seemed physical, as if I could hold them in my hands, and examine them from every angle. I was accepting that I didn't have all the answers and that I would never be able to explain why everything happened as it did. Eventually I began to acknowledge and own what had happened and focused instead on weaving myself together.

As I continued to write, I realized that I was hungry—not for food, but for information of all kinds. I emptied myself onto the page and needed to refill again. I became an intellectual omnivore, attending all kinds of classes: photography, history, Judaism, science, and religion. The more I interacted and exchanged information with other people, the better I felt. I still went to church—often with my fingers crossed as I recited the Apostles' and Nicene Creeds—but still attending. When Lent arrived, I signed up for a course at my church. There were more than a dozen of us, and we would be reading Thomas Moore's *The Care of the Soul*.

While in class I met a woman who felt, as I did, that the class had awakened a deep desire to continue to search for more answers. I suggested we start a women's spirituality group, because I wanted to examine my own soul, my core, to find out who I was.

She agreed, and we asked a few friends to join us. Soon six of us met twice monthly in the afternoons. We were all seeking to understand and expand our feminine spirituality. A year later, we decided we were brave enough to share our own histories with one another—"herstories" we called them—revealing our earliest memories and moving through grade school, high school, and beyond. Sharing these recollections led to investigations that took us several years.

As I revealed my life's experiences to my spiritual sisters, I began to appreciate how we all had struggled with the countless expectations we ourselves, our parents, and society had placed upon us. Then if we failed, which was a given, we isolated ourselves. Ashamed of our mistakes, we cut ourselves off from one another, from the very interactions that could comfort us the most. Reaching out to others often carried with it the threat of rejection. What held our healing also held our fears.

Lexa's Wedding

This above all: to thine own self be true, And
it must follow, as the night the day,
Thou canst not then be false to any man.

—*Shakespeare*

It was late one afternoon in June 2002, and I'd been back in Madison for almost three weeks when the phone rang. Lexa's voice skipped across the wires from Montana.

Mom, I have something to tell you. Her voice was filled with excitement.

Do I need to sit down? I said.

She laughed. You might want to.

Okay, what is it? I sat down in the nearest kitchen chair.

I've been engaged for two hours, with a ring, too, she exclaimed with delight.

Oh Lexa, that's wonderful. Tell me about it.

Stephen drove us out to where we'd had our first date—I told you we'd hiked in the foothills west of town.

Yes, I remember. It's so like you to be outdoors somewhere.

Well, anyway, we were on this little bench-like stump, and he handed me a box all tied up with colored ribbons. He said it was a journal for my poetry. Stephen wants me to start writing again, and the journal book was a hint. He started the first page for me, so I opened it up. He wrote that the last seven months had been the happiest times of his life. Two pages were stuck together, so I pried them open. On the page, he'd written "Will you marry me?"

That's terrific, I said, wishing I could be there to hug her.

Wait, there's more, she said. A hole was cut out in the middle of the pages, and in the hole was a little box. In the box was a gorgeous diamond ring.

How perfectly splendid! I asked if they'd set a date. Already my stomach was churning. I was hoping they would take their time. Mark and I hadn't been divorced that long, and I didn't think I could cope with a wedding just yet.

Well, we're thinking of a year from now, when Stephen's grad school is over, so it might be sometime next spring.

Wonderful, I said. I was relieved they weren't getting married immediately. With you working and Stephen's being in school, it'll take a while to bring things together, and you won't feel rushed.

I was on a teeter-totter of joy tinged with worry. A

marriage meant I'd have to see Lexa's father. I hadn't set eyes on Mark since before our divorce in December 2000. I didn't want to talk with him again.

We want to send out save-the-date cards as soon as we can, and we want Stephen's dad to do the ceremony—he's a judge.

I remembered Angela and Ethan's wedding, with Mark performing their marriage ceremony. Our lives had changed dramatically since then. Lexa probably wouldn't have chosen a church wedding anyway, I thought, so their decision to have Stephen's dad officiate seemed like the right one to me.

We started to discuss wedding details, while within, I was unnerved by the thought of having to see Mark again. I was looking forward to helping Lexa with her wedding plans. My relationship with her was so different than what my mom and I had had. I closed my eyes to keep from crying. I said a little prayer: I miss you, Mom. We'll do *this* wedding together, you and I...but I won't tell Lexa.

We're going to Stephen's parents' house for dinner tonight—we're telling them then, but I wanted you to know first. Her words whirred like a spinning wheel.

Lexa, will you come back here to Madison before you're married? I said.

That's the plan. We thought we'd come for a few days. I can show Stephen where we used to live and drive by the school, stuff like that, and maybe you and I can shop for some things.

That'll be fun. I love you, Lexa. Be happy. Enjoy your engagement time.

I will, Mom. I love you too.

The phone went silent. Engaged. My little girl. Suddenly I felt so alone—parents were supposed to share this kind of news. I picked up my Siamese cat, Meringue, and held her close.

I wanted to scream, This isn't fair. But I had stopped yelling a while ago. I gripped Meringue tighter. I wished I could call my parents, but they were dead. I ached with wanting to connect with some other person, to share the happy news.

Holding Meringue in my arms, I looked out the window at my garden. It was in full summer bloom: fat blue-violet hydrangeas, spunky yellow day lilies, and my mother's favorites—zinnias of every color, just like the ones I cut for her the summer before she died. There had been so much distance between us until the very end.

Lexa had already chosen her wedding gown—a surprise, she said. She still had to shop for the brides-maids' dresses.

June and July sped by while we planned the wedding using the Internet for quick communication. E-mails from Lexa arrived with many exclamation points and instructions about how to check out websites, how to see the dresses she liked.

Following her instructions, I scanned each dress and zinged back one of several replies: Not very flat-tering neckline. Color not great. Isn't that too sexy? That's good. Next?

I scooped up piles of bridal magazines, and we both bought a copy of the latest bridal etiquette book so we could refer to the same page. We set a budget based on our best guesses. Lexa kept track of every dollar we spent. She'd always been organized, and she was in her element as the days went by. For the ceremony, she and Stephen selected an outdoor setting near the Blackfoot River, not far from where they lived.

In mid-August, they came through Madison for a few days. Our first big decision was the bridesmaids' dresses. Lexa had narrowed down the color to a sage green similar to the green my bridesmaids had worn, but I didn't mention it. Was Lexa aware that her wedding date would be only ten days after mine? Despite my efforts not to think of him, I found myself replaying my own marriage to her father.

The day after Lexa and Stephen arrived, we visited a wedding shop. Lexa, as always, had done her homework. Walking directly to the rack that held every color green imaginable, she was looking for a long dress with an empire waist. For the next half-hour, she modeled bridesmaids' dresses for us. It was all Stephen could do to keep from yawning.

Try this, I said, handing her a pale green gown that had caught my eye.

Come in here, Mom, Lexa called from the dressing room. This dress is way too big for me.

Sure it is, but scrunch it up in the back, you'll get the idea, I said. One of the salespeople can pin it up for you.

Lexa and Stephen conferred about the bridesmaids' body types, hair colors, and complexions while I listened. Then I noticed a shawl that went perfectly with the last dress she modeled.

Look at this, I said.

Not bad, she said, flinging the shawl around her neck. But I didn't budget for this.

It's my gift to the bridesmaids, not to worry. What do you think?

I think it works, said Stephen, and giving a sigh of relief, he left to investigate some nearby art galleries while Lexa and I continued to shop.

We both tried on several pairs of shoes. Lexa tested each one with a little boogie in front of a skinny mirror. Walking arm in arm across the floor, we checked to see if we teetered on heels that were too high. It didn't take long to make our decisions. She picked elegant silk Mary Janes and I chose silver sling backs with sensible heels.

As we left the store I felt the moist, cool air moving in from the lake. There was one final purchase to make: the wedding veil. The streetlight changed from red to green, and Lexa started across the street just in front of me. She was wearing a pale blue t-shirt, khaki hiking shorts, and running shoes. Her forest-green backpack was slung over one shoulder. Perhaps that's what she wore the day she and Stephen became engaged.

We found the bridal salon and were greeted with a riot of gowns and veils of satin, silk, chiffon, and organdy overflowing the racks. Lexa marched straight to the counter. I want a short train, not a cathedral thing, she announced. Before I knew it, she was standing on a small box in the center of a platform surrounded by a triptych of mirrors.

Effortlessly, she wrapped her thick, long auburn hair into an updo. The saleswoman secured a veil to the back of her head. There she stood—in her t-shirt, shorts, and tennies—delicate ivory lace swirling around her pretty oval face, and a price tag dangling near her right ear. I felt in my purse for my camera. I'd left it in the car.

I laughed with tears in my eyes. Look at yourself, Lexa. Don't ever forget this moment. She turned away from the mirror and gazed at me whimsically. I knew then that she'd left home for good.

As we walked back to the parking lot, Lexa put her arm around me. Mom, did I ever thank you for not letting me watch MTV?

I can't remember, Lexa.

Well, I'm telling you now. When we have kids, we're not going to let them watch MTV either.

I smiled to myself as we got into the car.

଼

It was Labor Day 2002 when Lexa called me in the evening. I had returned to Tucson for the fall and winter. She spoke hurriedly and sounded pressured. She'd told her father that she was engaged to be married. Dad didn't offer to pay for any of the wedding expenses, she said.

I could hear the hurt in her voice and felt a stinging ache in the back of my throat. I tried to keep my frustration in check while I responded. Never mind. I've been planning for it. We've followed the budget we made together. Everything will be okay.

Are you sure? she gasped.

Of course. Don't worry about it. My words were crisp as cold celery.

We didn't speak of costs again, but we did have a grim time deciding on what wording to use for her wedding invitations. *Dr. and Mrs.* wouldn't work. And although there were lots of examples in the etiquette books, none fit our situation. I couldn't bring myself to list Mark as the host of Lexa's reception when he wasn't. But Lexa wanted her father's name on the invitation.

A week later, she called me to read what she decided for the invite. The mom's name goes first, she said. So your name, then "and" on the second line and Dad's name…

I interrupted her. You can't say that. That would mean both your dad and I are doing the inviting, and that's not correct.

Lexa raised her voice. Well, I know that, but how would *you* do it, then?

I'd leave him off. He's not the host. I'm the hostess. There *is* no host, Lexa.

But Stephen's parents' names will be on the invitation, and I want Dad's to be, too, she wailed.

Lexa, it can't be, I fired back. He's not giving the wedding reception. Angry tears filled my eyes. Weddings were occasions when families came together, but we weren't a family anymore. We'd been severed, and nothing was going to alter that.

Lexa and I were screeching at one another when Stephen interrupted on another phone. His voice was calm. I think we can work out something. It's about the inviting, isn't it?

Yes, I answered. I just can't do it. It's not right. It isn't true.

I can understand that. Believe me, I can. You know my parents were divorced, and I went through a lot of stuff like this. That's one of the reasons Lexa and I get along so well. We speak the same lingo about things that have happened in our families.

Well, you didn't have this problem, I spat back.

No, but I'm having it now.

Oh, right. I was startled by his subtle confrontation.

So, if it's the inviting part, can't we do something like you invite her dad and my parents to *join* with you...?

You are saying to write it like that?

Exactly. Your name, then the words "invites you to join her," then my parents' names and then her dad's and then "in celebrating the marriage of their children." You know the rest of it.

I guess that'd work. I took a deep breath and said, I'm sorry to be so touchy. I was embarrassed I'd been so stubborn.

It's okay, Mom, really. I understand, Lexa's voice chimed in.

I was glad we worked it out. She probably knew it was difficult for me to watch her approaching marriage when I hadn't healed from my own divorce. But I didn't think she knew how much I dreaded seeing her father.

℃

Lexa's wedding day was clear and in the seventies. If Mark and I had still been married, our thirty-eighth anniversary would have been ten days earlier. Lexa had given me a schedule of events, a list of places I was to be and what time to be there. All the guests had welcome baskets in their hotel rooms, where Lexa had left a note thanking them for coming. She had done more than plan a wedding; she had brought together extended families for a celebration.

I felt I was drifting through a well-rehearsed play: keep to my schedule, dress appropriately for the occasions, and show up at the appointed place on time. I was aware of the guests gathering and visiting, but I didn't stop to chat with them. I had to keep going. I still felt the sting of shame and humiliation that surrounded my divorce. Most of my friends knew the circumstances by this time, but I wondered if they thought I might be flustered or miss a cue. I wasn't going to. I refused to let anything spoil Lexa's wedding.

On Sunday morning, the bridesmaids and I were having brunch together in Lexa's hotel room while hairdressers were busily styling our hair. I got a glimpse of Lexa's life as she moved among her friends, laughing and happy. If she was nervous, she didn't show it.

We drove to the arboretum and went quickly to the room where we dressed for the ceremony. As I placed my grandmother's pearls around my neck, I was caught in a déjà vu. I had worn them years earlier at my own wedding. For a moment, I stared out the window, expecting to see the cathedral spire and the brilliant blue San Francisco Bay, but in the distance, I saw a river winding its way through the low hillside.

They're asking for you, Gale, I heard someone say. I took my long lavender silk dress from its hanger and let it slip over my head and shoulders. Looking in the mirror, I pinched my cheeks for more color and added a little more lipstick. Then I marched into the garden where the wedding party was gathered for photos. I smiled in all of them and returned to the dressing room to wait for the wedding to start. Kicking off my shoes, I balanced on a pile of pillows stacked on the window seat, closed my eyes, and tried to meditate. My stomach flipped, and I felt short of breath. Mark would be on Lexa's left. I wasn't going to look at him. I was here only for her.

Suddenly, the room was alive with young ladies in sage green who were adjusting straps and tugging at pantyhose. Lexa sat on a chair in the middle of the room while the bridesmaids wove stephanotis into her hairdo. One of the attendants gingerly handed the embroidered ivory wedding gown to Lexa, who—teetering on one foot and then the other—stepped into the dress and slipped its narrow ties over her slim shoulders. As she stood smiling in front of me, I swallowed my tears. Her sister-in-law, Angela, lifted the veil above Lexa's head and nestled the large comb into the top of her french twist.

Flashing through my mind was the picture of a three-year-old girl with long braids running out the kitchen door on her way to greet her grandfather. She was only three when my Dad had died. I missed him now, wishing he and Mom could see this day.

Let's all gather around Lexa and pray for her and Stephen as they begin their new life together this day as wife and husband, said Angela. We held hands and circled my daughter.

Within moments, the dressing room was empty. I stood there alone. A flash of panic swept through me. I swallowed hard. Not today, I said. Not now. I had to stay calm. I was going to walk Lexa down the aisle.

Lexa stood silhouetted in front of the large bay window surrounded by tables decorated with eucalyptus and candles. Mark was on the far side of her, partly hidden by her flowers and veil. I promised her a year ago that no matter what happened, I would be on her right side as she walked down the aisle. I felt tears pulsing behind my eyes.

Lexa held her bouquet in her left hand and stretching out her fingers, she touched my arm and said in a firm voice, Mom, take a deep breath. Another one. If you start crying, then I'll cry too.

Laughing and trembling, I opened my grandmother's evening purse and felt for the handkerchief inside. As I grasped it, I dug my nails into my palm. I'm okay. Don't worry, I said. I couldn't lose it now and embarrass my daughter.

Now listen, said Lexa. Here come the bagpipes. We stood on the patio at the top of the path as the piper walked down the grass aisle to the flower-covered trellis and stood to one side behind the groomsmen. The bridesmaids followed.

Here we go, said Lexa.

You set the pace. I'll follow your lead. I placed my hand under her arm.

The photos show us with smiles on our faces. People said we looked like sisters. I must have floated down the aisle, because I couldn't remember how I got there. Lexa stopped, grinned at Stephen, and turned to give me a kiss.

God bless, I whispered, stepping back to take my seat.

Lexa and Stephen had written the ceremony. The words they exchanged were a combination of traditions and their own beliefs and dreams. All too quickly, it was over, and guests were following the bride and groom up the aisle. I spotted Ethan standing near the door. He opened his arms to me. Suddenly Lexa joined us, and all three of us were using my handkerchief.

Mark and I were seated on either side of the dining room with our backs to each other, so we couldn't see one another unless we turned around. There were several toasts, a good deal of dancing, and much laughter. Before the cake was cut, Lexa and Stephen visited at each table. As the cake was served, I thanked our guests for joining us on this special day. I was tired, but no panic attack had ruined the day. I caught a glimpse of Mark across the room, but our eyes didn't meet. Seeing him wasn't as hard as I thought it would be.

Later I realized that in his own way, Ethan had filled in for his dad that day. He was the perfect host. He mingled with family and friends and checked in with me several times during the evening. Our family relationships had shifted. There were new roles for everyone.

Lexa and Stephen gave their guests sparklers to use as a send-off signal. They twinkled in the shadowed patio as the married couple walked down the path to the waiting car. The guests waved and wished them well.

A few weeks later, after I had returned to Madison, I received a phone call from one of my good friends. She wanted to know if I had seen Mark dancing with a man at Lexa's reception, but I hadn't.

Well, I was thinking he really did you a favor.

What do you mean?

The guests there could see him, so now it's hardly a secret anymore what the problem was.

I guess you're right. I hadn't thought of it that way. His preferring men was the ghost that haunted our marriage for thirty-five years, the secret he kept from everyone. Even our counselors never said anything. I paused a moment to think and then said, I don't know why I didn't see it back then, not that I would have wanted to.

Well, that's the point; we don't see what we don't want to see.

I seem to remember that, now that you mention it. Good old denial. Sometimes a friend; sometimes an enemy.

The Glass Ceiling

> Blessed are the poor in spirit, for theirs is the
> kingdom of God. Matt 5:3. They have a big
> head start over the rest of us, because God's
> privileged and often hidden position is at the
> bottom and edge of things, never at the top
> or center.
>
> —*Richard Rohr*

The phone call I had just received about Mark caught
me off guard, reminding me that I needed to get in
touch with Melissa Carr, my attorney. I had decided to
put aside my disagreement with the diocesan bishop
until after Lexa's wedding, but now it was time for me
to hear how Melissa planned for us to proceed.

Two years earlier, in spring 2001, when Mark had
been suspended from holy orders, I had asked the
bishop for an annulment or whatever its equivalent
was in the Episcopal Church. He told me he could not
do that for me. I was furious and spent a month trying

to find a lawyer, since most of Madison's law firms represented some segment of the Episcopal diocese. I thought an attorney might be better equipped to get the bishop's attention than I was. With the help of a good friend with legal experience, I was able to contact Melissa Carr, an attorney in a small firm.

My divorce was final in December 2000. However, I had two concerns about my marital status that specifically involved my church, not the court. The first was my personal need for my church to recognize that I had no ties to my former husband. I wanted to be recognized as a *single* woman in the eyes of the church. It was my way of trying to erase Mark from my life. The second was the result of the church canons, or laws, which made it clear that because I was a divorceé, if I ever wanted to remarry in the Episcopal Church, I would have to have a bishop's permission to do so. I thought my church was out of date.

When Melissa and I first met, back in July 2001, she quickly determined that we needed the advice of a person skilled in Episcopal canon law. I made several phone calls to clergy friends across the country asking for referrals until I found the right person, Betty Burton. Melissa asked Betty to research situations that were similar to mine. It was a slow process, and there wasn't much available. Halloween was fast approaching before the three of us met to compile our evidence and plan our presentation. Melissa had been successful in making an early-November appointment with the diocesan bishop.

By this time, both Melissa and I had bought the

book *Constitutions and Canons 2000*, and I found the section on canon law that applied to divorce, clearly spelled out in Title I, Canon 19.

> Sec. 2 (a) Any member of this Church whose marriage has been annulled or dissolved by a civil court may apply to the Bishop or Ecclesiastical Authority of the Diocese in which such person is legally or canonically resident for a judgment as to his or her marital status in the eyes of the Church. Such judgment may be a recognition of the nullity, or of the termination of the said marriage; Provided, that no such judgment shall be construed as affecting in any way the legitimacy of children or the civil validity of the former relationship. (b) Every judgment rendered under this Section shall be in writing and shall be made a matter of permanent record in the Archives of the Diocese.

Reading this, it seemed to me that my bishop could give me what I wanted if he chose to do so. What was holding him back?

The day of our meeting arrived one year after I'd first met with the bishop about Mark. Melissa had instructed me not to say anything unless she or the bishop asked me a question. She would present the situation as we saw it, and I would watch on the sideline. Betty was there as backup in case any canon law was discussed. As we entered the meeting room, the bishop shook hands with each of us. The ceiling was high, and the room was poorly lit. Heavy velvet drapes framed the oversized windows. Several straight-back chairs stood in place around an oversized antique wooden table. I felt as if I'd stepped back to the time of the Inquisition. The canon advocate, Betty, explained her legal background in canon law and said she was there as a resource person for Melissa and me.

Melissa began her presentation. She emphasized that there were three persons involved in the situation—the bishop, Mark, and me—forming a triangle with the bishop at the top as the representative of the Episcopal Church. She said that the relationship between the bishop and Mark had been altered due to his suspension. He was no longer allowed to function as a priest, so his position was clear. Then she stated that the relationship between Mark and me was also obvious: we had been severed by divorce almost a year earlier.

But what is the relationship between the church and Gale, who is a member of the Episcopal Church in this diocese? Melissa said as she looked directly at the bishop.

The bishop folded his hands together on his lap and then, shifting in his chair, admitted he had not given much thought to an annulment after he had met with Mark earlier that April. Melissa pressed forward, stating that it seemed his decision placed more value on Mark's statement of intent to commit to the marriage than to my litany of examples of how Mark had failed to commit to the marriage. Slowly uncrossing his legs, the bishop pushed himself a few inches back from the table. The grandfather clock behind me ticked off the minutes. His hand reached for the large gold cross on his chest. When he finally spoke, he proposed that he write another letter to me, one using different phrases, which might be more acceptable to me. Then you could look it over and reply with suggestions, he said, gazing just over my head.

But I didn't want that. I want the annulment equivalent, I said under my breath, having promised Melissa I'd hold my tongue in front of the bishop.

Suddenly the bishop got up and headed to the door. He nodded at the three of us. My momentary absence will give you ladies some time to talk, he said.

Melissa frowned as he closed the door behind him. She said we ought to take his offer and run with it, and then added; at least I could craft something that was legitimate.

But I want an annulment. This time I said it aloud to Melissa and Betty.

We'll get there, but it may take a while, Melissa said and turned to Betty. What do you think?

Betty had been silent throughout the meeting. Now she said, I'd take his suggestion and then see what happens. This problem isn't going to be resolved soon. You can see how closed he is.

I told you he would be. I sighed. I was tired and felt dismissed.

Well, let's take it, then. It's disappointing, but at least we have a starting point, said Melissa. It'll also give Betty some more time to research the issue.

When the bishop returned, Melissa thanked him

for his time and said we'd look forward to receiving his letter.

It was not until January 2002, two months after we had met with the bishop, that I received his promised letter. It held no reference to an annulment. He did disclose that Mark had admitted to the violations of his marriage vows and that they had begun early in our marriage, which raised questions about his commitment and intent. The bishop made it clear that the Church did not condone Mark's behavior. He said that he would pray for my children and me and that if I wanted to be remarried in the Church, I would have his support to do so.

If the Church didn't condone Mark's behavior, then why couldn't I be granted an annulment?

The following day I called Melissa about the bishop's letter idea and asked her what she and Betty planned to do next. I was getting ready to call you about that, Melissa said. Then she explained that she had tried to get in touch with Betty by phone and e-mail but had not received any reply. I told her that I, too, had phoned Betty several times at her work number, as well as her secure number, but there was no answer. Neither of us ever heard from her again, although much later we were assured she had never left her job.

Melissa listened while I voiced my irritation with the bishop. I reminded her that I would be leaving soon to spend the winter in Arizona. She said she would like some more time to think through what had happened. I said I was going to speak to some of my clergy friends in other dioceses to ask what they thought of the pushback I was getting from my bishop. None approved of the way my request was being handled. All of them urged me to continue my efforts to be heard.

Then one Sunday, about two months after I'd received my bishop's resounding no, I was browsing in my parish bookstore in Arizona when I picked up a book by Bishop John Shelby Spong, the then bishop of Newark, titled *Here I Stand*. As I was leafing through it, I came upon "The Statement of Koinonia." It was a declaration written by Bishop Spong, which he presented to the House of Bishops during the Episcopal General Convention in Indianapolis the summer of 1994. He proclaimed that both homosexuality and heterosexuality were morally neutral, and as such, he affirmed his support for ordination of homosexuals in the Episcopal Church. He went on to state that both orientations had the ability to live their sexuality in destructive or positive ways. Reading it through, I noted at the end that several bishops whom I knew had also signed the statement. I thought I'd found important information that would oblige the diocesan bishop to grant me the annulment. I bought the book and took it home to study further.

The following day I phoned Melissa and carefully explained what I had found. My bishop can't have it both ways, I said. Listen to this: "We believe that wherever sexuality is lived out destructively, this Church must witness to its negativity. We oppose all forms of promiscuous sex, predatory sex, and sex that does not honor one's partner or sex that does not hold that partner in commitment and love." Bishop Spong—

he's the bishop of New Jersey—wrote that, and my bishop signed the document, along with eighty-seven other bishops in the Episcopal Church. I've got Spong's book right in front of me. If my bishop believes what he signed, then he *has* to grant me the equivalent of an annulment!

That's quite something, she said. I have to agree with you. Can you send me the references? It may be time for you to write to the next authority in the diocese.

You mean the standing committee? I knew every diocese had a committee that served to advise diocesan bishops.

They're the next step up, aren't they? she said.

I think that's how it works. The only people, or person really, that's higher up would be the presiding bishop, and his office is in New York.

Let's start with the standing committee, then.

Will you send a cover letter? With your firm's heading on it, they'll at least read it, I said.

Absolutely. Call me when you have something for me to read.

I'll just tell them what happened. I said. I sat down at my computer and wrote what had unfolded to date between my bishop and me. I shared some of my growing concerns:

The Episcopal Diocese has been in denial around many issues involving sexuality and thus has avoided looking at the seriousness of and the ramifications of the terrible wrongdoings in the area of sexual misconduct by clergy. I know that this priest (my ex-husband) is not the only clergy person in this diocese who has been deposed or suspended for violation of Title IV, Canon 2 Section 1, but I fear that given the denial and general attitude toward this situation there may well be a great deal more that is being swept under the table. If anything at all should be happening at this time, it is a thorough soul searching. Certainly, the Episcopal Church ought not to be complacent in view of what is happening within the Roman Church, and surely its various bodies of leadership cannot be so naïve as to believe that the Episcopal Church is exempt from similar difficulties.

When I first went to my bishop in November of 2000, I'd never heard of Title IV. After obtaining the book *Constitutions and Canons 2000* in 2001, Melissa and I examined it carefully. As I read more of Title IV, particularly Canon 3, I began to realize that *I* might be considered a person (the words *victim* and *complainant* were used in the canon) who was bringing a complaint against a clergy person. Canon 3 Section 4 ended with, "Any alleged Victim or Complainant shall also be entitled to the counsel of an attorney and/or Advocate of their choice." I made it clear in my letter to the committee that at *no* time had my bishop suggested that he might appoint a suitable attorney and/or an advocate to assist me as I brought my story to him.

I ended my letter with the following sentence:

Healing from betrayal and violation of both spirit and person, at the hands of anyone, but particularly someone in Holy Orders, is the core business of the Church, and yet, somehow the Church continues to turn its back on the very persons that Christ called us to minister to.

Melissa attached her cover letter to mine, having written:

I represent [Gale Harris] as she pursues closure to having been sexually victimized by one of your Episcopal priests (her ex-husband) throughout her marriage. (This priest is canonically resident in the Episcopal Diocese.) At this time, all Ms. Harris is asking is that the Episcopal Church nullify her marriage as provided for by Title I, Canon 19 § 2(a). It is my professional opinion, after reviewing state law, federal law, and Episcopal Canon Law, that it is in the best interest of all parties concerned to grant Ms. Harris's request without further delay.

Melissa ended her letter by explaining that Mark's statement, which he left in our home, was the "biography of a man who never intended to commit to his marriage, despite his contrary statement to the bishop. Mr. M.'s [Mark's] admitted conduct belies the integrity of his words."

So there would be no misunderstanding, Melissa made reference to Mark's predatory behavior and then commented, "In refusing to nullify a marriage so flawed in its inception, the Episcopal Church appears to be more concerned about protecting its priests (like the Catholic Church) than its victims."

I was grateful that Melissa had been so clear about what had happened.

It was midsummer 2002 when my letter, accompanied by Melissa's cover letter, was sent to the standing committee. In order to keep all conversations transparent, she sent copies to the bishop and his chancellor as well. Within days, the president of the committee phoned Melissa to tell her that a separate meeting would be held to discuss the matters that my statement raised.

At first, I felt hopeful, but as the hot summer weeks passed with no reply, I began to lose faith in ever being heard by my church. It was the end of July when Melissa finally received a reply to her cover letter. The committee had supported the bishop's previous stand on my "nullity issue."

Melissa said she wanted to review some of the canon law we had been studying for months. She said that she needed time to think through the use of words.

I have an idea, she said. I'm not a canon lawyer, but law is law, and words and how they are used are important. I'll get back to you by the end of the week.

Words, yes, she was right. They were important, as a messenger of the truth, and protectors of secrets and misinformation. I'd been dealing with words for decades: Mother's, Mark's, and the church's. Naming things correctly and telling the ultimate truth were challenging.

On Friday morning, Melissa called me. I don't know if this is it, but I'd like your permission to try something. I think the word *annulment* bugs your bishop. I'd like to write to the president of the standing committee again and see what happens. I want to emphasize your connection with your church and forget the word annulment for a minute. I want them to focus on the particular relationship, your marriage, which doesn't exist anymore, and what the church names *that* death. Does it renounce it or recognize it?

I understand what you are saying, I answered. I guess we have to see if the committee and the bishop get it. I was reminded how a single word can transform a lifetime.

By summer's end, we'd heard nothing from the committee. Melissa told me she was going to call the diocesan chancellor's office to make an appointment. Perhaps he would meet with her, attorney to attorney.

Within thirty-six hours, Melissa received an e-mail from the committee president explaining that her letter of early August would be on the committee's agenda in its upcoming meeting following Labor Day. The same day Melissa received that e-mail, the bishop wrote a letter to me stating he was inclined to agree with Melissa that some misunderstanding about the wording of my request might have occurred.

It infuriated me that the bishop stonewalled for two years, rebuffing and obstructing my attempts to obtain an annulment. All he needed to say was, Let me explain. I can't nullify your marriage. For me to do that, you would have needed an annulment in civil court. You had a divorce. What I can consider, however, is what Title I, Canon 19 states is a "judgment of your marital status" in the eyes of the Church.

It was October 10, 2002, when I finally received the official Judgment of Termination and was once again an unmarried woman in the eyes of my church. Thank God my connection to Mark had been severed in every way possible. I felt relieved that my efforts had been rewarded. However, the two years of struggling with the bishop and his toying with me because of the one word—annulment—didn't sit well with me. I felt manipulated, fragmented, and unwilling to simply accept all the anguish I went through with the bishop and the church. It didn't seem justified to me. And what about others who might have to go through the same thing? I decided to call Melissa. My frustration spilled out as I spoke.

Melissa, if an attorney had been with me the first time I met the bishop back in November 2000, that entire meeting would have had a different feel. An attorney would have commented about Mark's behavior and inquired about notifying the civil authorities. I don't want to sound spiteful, but I want the truth.

Yes, you're probably right about that—although, it may have been something the lawyer would have discussed later, not in your presence, she said.

That's true. It was my assumption that the bishop would do the right thing, not only for Mark, but also for my children and me. If an attorney had been there, you for instance, you would have inquired what justice I might obtain in the eyes of my church. This craziness of my needing to find a canon advocate to tell me how to get the equivalent of an annulment was absurd. The church should have been reaching out to me. I shouldn't have to beg my church for help. I trusted the bishop to hold my husband accountable and help my children and me. Now I think the bishop needs to be held responsible. I held my breath as I waited to hear her reaction.

I know you're distressed. It's been a tough two years. Are you certain you still want to pursue it? Do you want to bring a charge against the bishop?

I have to. What happened was wrong. I don't think the committee registered that the bishop failed to advise me of my rights under canon law. It's all right there in Title IV, Canon 3. The bishop has finally given me the marital judgment; that's true. But what about my complaint about Mark's behavior toward our children and me? The bishop never mentioned anything about my rights to counsel. And of course, I didn't know I had any rights under canon law until you and I started reading about them. Not many people are going to do that.

Well, I agree. I'll review Canon IV again, and I want you to do the same. By the way, are you aware of what's going on with the Roman Church in Boston?

Oh yes. I'm afraid it sounds familiar—the culture of arrogance and secrecy. That's one of the reasons I want to pursue this. Rome isn't the only institution that's sitting on secrets.

Early in 2002, the *Boston Globe* reported that child sexual abuse was a common problem in the

Roman Catholic Archdiocese of Boston. More than a year later, when I returned to Madison for the summer, instances of child exploitation were surfacing throughout the world. Everywhere I turned, I heard and read of people's accusations and disbelief, sorrow, and fury— the same feelings I had.

A gnawing discontent and uneasiness crawled through my body, followed almost immediately by the horrible recognition of a familiar monster. I hated to think that my own church might be covering for its clergy too.

It was early June 2003 when Melissa and I decided that the time had come for me to write to the presiding bishop of the Episcopal Church, headquartered in New York City. If he were willing to hear my story, maybe some mending could occur. I wrote to the presiding bishop—as well as his assistant, the bishop in charge of pastoral direction—asking him to explain why my bishop had neglected to tell me that I could have had an attorney represent me. It seemed to me I was bringing a complaint against a clergy person, though at the time I didn't know this process was addressed by canon law.

After a year of many unanswered phone calls between Melissa and the presiding bishop's chancellor, a decision was finally reached. In mid-November 2004, Melissa flew from Madison to Tucson. Together we greeted the pastoral bishop and a social worker, Ms. Rhodes, who had come from New York to meet with Melissa and me at my church.

As we all walked into the meeting room, the pastoral bishop took off his jacket and tossed it over the nearest chair. He wore, of course, a magenta colored shirt reserved for bishops in the Episcopal Church. I watched as he reached for the small wooden cross he wore. He stuffed it into his shirt pocket. I believed the pastoral bishop was signaling me that he had a distinctly different intent in mind than the bishop of my diocese. I sensed that we would have an honest and personal conversation together, not one based on "holiness" and canon laws.

He introduced himself and made it clear that both he and Ms. Rhodes were members of the Task Force on Title IV, the canon law pertaining to "conduct unbecoming of clergy." We've been working with a group for several years, trying to get Title IV more user-friendly. It's slow going.

He pulled up a chair and motioned to us to sit down as well. I would like to hear your story. He took no notes. He told me to be frank with him, emphasizing that he wanted to hear *exactly* what I had experienced. It took me more than an hour to tell him what had occurred in my family. Often I closed my eyes and tried to visualize the exact scene to find the precise words. I told him that I couldn't seem to make my bishop understand how much I hurt. He leaned forward in his chair. Who first comforted you when you found that document you brought to your bishop?

I replied that one of my close woman friends had driven me to the bishop's office.

And after that, who helped you when you wrestled with the shock and anger?

No one really. But I was seeing a therapist.

No clergy person was working with you then?
Melissa and Ms. Rhodes both sat quietly.

No, no clergy, I said.

I'm sorry you and your family didn't receive proper pastoral care at the time. How do you think you're doing now?

I told him more about my counselor and my Al-Anon group.

Are you making progress, then?

I said I thought so, except for all the trouble with my bishop. I said I didn't think he had handled Mark's and my situation very well. Ms. Rhodes mentioned she'd like to keep in touch with me for a while, to follow how I was doing, and I responded I was agreeable with that.

It was months before I could unravel what I had felt that day with the pastoral bishop. What occurred was almost like a confessional. The pastoral bishop, Melissa, and Ms. Rhodes were compassionate witnesses to my pain. They heard my story. It was what I had to give to them. They accepted me. I felt I had been purified. In time, this led to my being able to accept myself, with all my anxieties, my denial, and my mistakes.

After a brief break to walk about and have a cup of coffee, the pastoral bishop and Ms. Rhodes explained how the church had been working for a decade to revise Title IV to make it relevant to today's world—more specific and transparent. A new version of Title IV had been outlined, and they hoped it would be ready for a vote the summer of 2006 at the Episcopal General

Convention in Columbus, Ohio. The pastoral bishop asked me if I would read it over and send him my suggestions. He said he wanted to take those ideas to the committee, which was scheduled to meet early in 2005. It was encouraging to know that the church law was being revised.

It was almost dark when we finished. I was gathering together my shoulder bag and papers when I realized Ms. Rhodes wanted to talk to me. I thought I heard her say, Pray for your diocese.

As I continued to learn about healing, I realized that the day with the pastoral bishop had been a pivotal time for me. Before—in November 2000, when I had first met with my own bishop—I was in shock, scared and angry. What I really needed most of all then was compassion and understanding. When he remarked that the written material I had found in Mark's den was "just gay porn," he had cut me to the core. I lost faith in my church that day. Now I wanted the assurance that no one would ever be treated in such an arrogant manner again.

I took Melissa to her hotel and thanked her for all her help along the way. Driving home early that evening, I felt a relief and freedom I hadn't experienced before. Nonetheless, I worried that even if the new canons were passed in June 2006, each diocese would have to choose to implement them. How that would happen remained to be seen.

It's Been a Long Time Since I've Seen You

You can't give away what you don't have.
—*Deepak Chopra*

My life was shifting, and I began to look beyond my computer screen. I decided to call a former English teacher to tell her I was writing a memoir. I thought you'd be surprised, I said.

On the contrary. I just wondered when you were going to get started, she replied.

I stored away her words just as I did when I was a student in her high-school English class. If she thought I could do it, then I would. Replaying her words now, I'm tempted to say she knew perfectly well the kind of pilgrimage I was undertaking. I didn't realize it at the time, of course, but writing a memoir would require a thorough investigation of my own soul and spirit.

It was early May 2004. My women's group was still meeting twice monthly. This week it was my turn to share material—part of my own "herstory"—and I was planning to tell my spiritual sisters that I was going to meet Deborah, my birth daughter. Only a few people knew that I had placed a newborn baby for adoption. She was coming to Arizona for Mother's Day, so I wanted to share my excitement, as well as my trepidation, with them.

I arrived early at the church where some of us were members. We met in what was called the bride's room. I had pictures of Deborah with me, and when we all were seated in a circle, I started to pass them around. This is my other daughter, I said. My birth daughter.

I told them about meeting Richard when I was just eighteen, how I'd gotten carried away by him and, not incidentally, pregnant as well. As I listened to my matter-of-fact presentation, I realized I had almost succeeded in erasing the ache of that experience—as if Deborah could be cut out of my life like a paper doll. Not so easy. Every year, when her birthday came around, I said a silent prayer, hoping she was alive, hoping she was well and happy. She was always there beside me, a complicated memory: dark hair peeking out from the pink blanket a nurse held in her arms as she rushed her to the newborn nursery. I never got to hold her. That wasn't allowed in the late fifties.

The responses I got to my story were sensitive and kind. They all spoke at once and wanted to hear everything about her. I really don't have much more to share,

I said. Only her letters and photos. I'll know more after we've had a weekend together.

Driving home that afternoon after our meeting, I shouted aloud: Free at last, God Almighty, free at last! I hadn't realized until then how heavily my secret had weighed on my heart all those years. My mind traveled back to the first time I had heard from Deborah.

It was a lazy fall day in 1985. Mark and I had been in our new home in Madison for only a few months. I was watching the Canada geese on our nature lake practicing takeoffs and landings for the winter migration when the kitchen phone rang. I picked it up.

Was there anything unusual that happened in your life early in 1959? I heard a young woman's voice say.

I knew right away that it was her. I've been expecting your call for quite a while. I glanced over my shoulder to see if Lexa was within earshot. Ethan was away at school, and Mark wasn't home yet.

You have? She sounded breathless.

Sure. That's why I put my real name on your birth certificate.

That certainly made it easier, she said in a clipped tone.

Her name was not what I would have chosen, but that wasn't my decision to make. She called because she was planning to have children and wanted to check out my family's medical history. I was surprised that her parents hadn't received those details when she was adopted. We talked cautiously back and forth for a short while. I asked if she would send me a photo of herself.

Should I just put my return address on the envelope—no name above it?

That's fine, I said.

Is it all right if I call you again? Maybe I could write a letter, too? she said.

Yes, of course. Please do. Then I quickly added. Maybe calling in the evenings would be better.

Tied up with mixed emotions, grateful yet rattled, I didn't know what else to say. As I hung up the phone, tears streamed down my face. I let out the breath I'd been holding for years. She'd made it! My firstborn baby girl was alive and well and going to have a child of her own. I was curious: Did she have nice parents? Where did she live? What did she do? Did she look like her father or me? I had to wait until she wrote me to find out. I didn't want to impose on her. At the time, I would never have tried to find her, but now that years have passed and I've learned more about being a birth mother, I wish she'd found me sooner than she did.

After dinner, while Mark and I were cleaning up the kitchen, I told him about my phone call from Deborah. He looked at me vaguely, as if trying to remember who she was. It was so like him to be distant and removed, somewhere else in his head and not with me.

I celebrated Deborah's entering my life, after twenty-six years, by myself. That was okay with me. After all, I'd brought her into the world alone; why should her reemergence be any different? I'd forgotten to ask her if she'd tried to find her father. I figured he wouldn't want to see her, and I didn't want her to be hurt.

When I first received Deborah's photo, I recognized her instantly. She looked exactly like her dad: oval face, dark brown eyes, Roman nose, deep-brown hair. She could have been her father's twin sister. She had my mother's natural curls. Deborah was just a little older than her father was when I last saw him—at his college graduation in 1958.

Now that I had met her through her photo, I was immediately concerned about her. When we next spoke, I posed questions: If anything awful happened to her, if she were to get terribly ill, or if she were in an accident and died, would her parents tell me? She said she'd already told her mother what to do in case of emergency and had given her parents my contact information.

I'm not going to die for some time, though, so you don't need to worry, she said.

She was like that—up front, on target, and always ahead of me. I asked if our conversations were okay with her parents. She told me they were delighted and had encouraged her to find me if she wished. Her parents knew more about me now. I wasn't a secret for them, but she was still *my* secret.

Deborah wanted to meet me as soon as possible, but I hadn't informed either of my children about her yet, although I had been planning to tell Ethan sometime soon. He was eighteen and headed for college. Lexa was only eight, and I didn't feel comfortable telling her then that she had a half-sister. I felt like a hostess without a guestroom. I wasn't quite prepared to welcome Deb into my family of four.

We began a twenty-year exchange of letters, eventually making the segue to e-mails. I read her letters when I was home alone. She was still a secret, and I didn't want to get too close, afraid that I'd experience again the absence of all those years.

By the time the millennium approached, we had shared a lot of our lives with each other. We were both graduates of the University of California at Berkeley. She had a daughter from her first marriage and had been divorced a few years later. She married again and had two boys. As we continued building our friendship, we discussed moments about motherhood but skipped over the heavy-duty discussions: What's it like to give away your baby, and its corollary, What's it like to be given away?

Now, two decades after that first phone call, Deborah would be arriving tomorrow. When I arrived home from my meeting, I readied my guestroom for her and placed a toy bear, the UC mascot dressed in blue and gold, on the pillow. As I stood back looking at the bed, I wondered what it might have been like if I had had a family with three children.

That evening Deborah called. I told my mom that I was scared, she said. She reminded me that you were a mother and that if I was having any trouble, she was certain you could help me out. My mom told me to tell you that.

I can't remember if I ever told Deb what a brave, selfless mother she had.

The next morning, I drove along the desert highway to the airport. The saguaro cacti, with crowns of small

white flowers on their prickly tops, lined each side of
the road. There was a tiny, hard knot in my stomach. I
felt uneasy, turned inside out. A stranger was going to
be spending the night. She's not really a stranger, I kept
telling myself. She's your daughter. What will we talk
about? What if she doesn't like me? What if I don't like
her?

The escalator glided down toward me. She was
dressed in white jeans and a bright blue tank top. A tote
bag hung over her shoulder. Our eyes met. She handed
me a bouquet—a giant red rose surrounded with ferns
and baby's breath. Happy Mother's Day, she said.

We cautiously hugged one another.

She grinned. It's been a long time since I've seen
you. I brought tons of pictures to share. There's hardly
room in my bag for any clothes, said Deb.

I recognized her big smile and intense dark eyes.
Deborah wasn't a photo anymore, but a real person.

She stared at me. Are you okay?

Yes...I'm just a bit overwhelmed. I couldn't take
my eyes off her.

Me too. Oh, there's my bag. She walked quickly to
the moving carousel and pointed to the one with the
Cal colors on it.

I see it. I spotted the blue and gold ribbons, our
alma mater's colors. I thought it was curious that we'd
both graduated from the same university.

On the way to my house, she told me about her
daughter, Victoria. She's looking at colleges now, said
Deb. How close is the university campus here?

About twenty minutes that way, I said, nodding to

the north. Just below the nook in those mountains. I can drive right by it on the way. I felt like I'd known her forever, yet I was aware of a great vacant space between us. All those absent years.

She rattled off her sentences. I can take some pictures for her. It's certainly spacious here. She has a friend here a year ahead of her, and Victoria might come for a visit before she applies.

Our weekend together had begun. I knew she was nervous, but then so was I. We both seemed to accept that we had "known" one another since the beginning and took for granted that there was a fundamental trust between us. We talked away half the night.

When I awoke the next morning, I saw the snapshots of Lexa, Ethan, and my brother and his family on my chest of drawers. Suddenly it struck me that the young woman in my home was related to all of them. Overnight, she'd slipped into another context—my life and everyone in it. Previously we had existed as a dyad that only we had access to. Now we were both part of a larger world, connected to people we had yet to meet.

We had a lifetime to share with one another. There wasn't enough time to catch up in just three days—it would take the rest of our lives. The weekend whirled away, and soon we were packing up our photos. Throughout our time together, we discussed the important people in our lives and what they meant to us. It was like getting acquainted with all the characters in a Shakespearian play. What we missed, we left unsaid.

Soon I was driving her back to the airport. We chattered all the way. Silence wasn't a word in our vocabulary. As we approached the boarding area, Deborah turned to hug me good-bye. She gave me a long look and then, with the beautiful grin on her face that I'd become accustomed to, Thanks for having me, she said.

My pleasure. I waved good-bye to her until she disappeared in a crowd of passengers.

We stayed in touch using e-mail and talked for hours on the phone late at night. It seemed the natural thing to do now, to share the everyday happenings of our lives with each other. I told her about my dating experiences.

It's been difficult, I said. It's like being twenty all over again, with the same kinds of questions, you know: what to wear, who pays for dinner, what will we talk about. I'm no good at small talk.

Of course you are. So am I. We're both like that, but do you want to have just small talk?

No, but you have to start somewhere. What do I do if I'm bored?

How about just excusing yourself and leaving?

That sounded so sensible as she said it. But I couldn't do that.

Sure, you could. You're never going to see the guy again anyway.

You're right, I guess. She was one smart lady.

I'm just kidding you. I know it's hard. I had it sort of easy when I married the second time. We both worked in the same building.

That's just it—there's no place to meet people, not

when you're my age and a grandmother. After all, I'm a sixty-year-old mother with two grown children, well three actually, who're older than I was the last time I dated. Frankly, I'm scared, and sometimes I'm just tired of thinking about it. I know what I want. It's what I didn't have: a committed relationship with a straight man. She was easy to talk to. I couldn't talk that way with Lexa and Ethan.

That's understandable. You'll have that, but not until you're in the right place with yourself, she replied.

Deborah had nailed my challenge: I wasn't whole yet. I didn't know it then, but I wasn't ready for any kind of a relationship, let alone a serious one. However, I'd met Colin, a man who seemed to be right, and I so wanted to believe I was secure enough to make a good choice.

During one of my phone chats with Deb, I got the nerve to explain that I was in a serious relationship. I mentioned I was a little worried that he might depend too much on an after-dinner drink or two or three. I was attending Al-Anon and was still worried about having someone around to ward off my anxiety attacks. I hadn't had a bad panic attack in several years, but I still thought about them. Some of the arguments I got into with Colin were similar to those I'd had with Mark—a lot of emotional distance between us.

He can't be present with you if he's already committed to something else, said Deb.

I know that, I said, bypassing her comment. I did one thing right, though—he's a straight man.

That may be, she shot back. But he's not being honest with you.

He isn't nice to my cats, I admitted. He pulls their tails.

You let him do that?

Her words were stinging in my ears. I didn't answer. I was ashamed, afraid I might have lost her respect.

She continued. Remember, I've already done that for us. I told you I divorced the alcoholic in my life. You don't need to go through that too.

I spent time thinking about what I told her and how sensible she was. I'd break it off with Colin. I'd be better off alone than battling with a relationship that was, in some ways, a remake of Mark and me.

She phoned me the day after I reported he'd gone. What are you going to do if he calls?

I guess I won't answer his call.

Her voice was sharp. Guess? Just call me if you want someone to talk to!

Deborah was going to make me toe the line. Undoubtedly, Ethan and Lexa saw the same unhappy situation, but it isn't easy to intervene with a parent. There was no way I could get around Deb. Besides, I knew she was right. I had gotten myself into another dependent relationship. The next time Colin called, I didn't answer. I put a star on my refrigerator instead. It was hard for a while. But I got used to being on my own again, and my anxiety calmed down too.

There was, however, something I never got a chance to thank Colin for. One night, as I began to fill with apprehension, I felt a cool sensation flow through my body just before I struggled to breathe. I told him that I thought I was having a panic attack. I had always tried to hide my attacks, but not this time.

I can rub your back, he said, and began to do so. I started to relax and forced myself to breathe very slowly. I almost held my breath. The attack started to resolve itself. I realized that I was learning how to let go instead of tightening up as an attack began. Recognizing that sensation, I realized I had less concern about my anxiety than before. I was profoundly grateful for the help Colin unknowingly gave me.

CB

On my way through the Bay Area in June 2004, I stopped by to visit Deborah. She had invited me to meet her children and husband. I had studied their photos and immediately recognized them. We had dinner together, and I slipped into their family as though it was something I did every Wednesday evening. Her middle child—Dylan, fourteen—played the piano for me. Her daughter—Victoria, sixteen—teased her youngest brother—Todd, ten—who was shy and asked if he could be excused from the table to do his homework.

It wasn't until I was outside walking down the stairs to my car that I felt overwhelmed. I tried to gulp down my tears. I had just grasped the fact that I'd met my grandchildren! All your wonderful kids, all at once. I'm just not used to this, I sputtered.

Oh, just think of them as bonus babies, Deb said casually as she put her arm around my waist to steady me. They've known about you for a long time. I told them when they were very young that I had another family, one I didn't know much about. They're good kids. They like you. I can tell, Deb said as she opened my car door.

Bonus babies, I thought to myself as I drove away. So, the world sometimes comes with bonus babies.

Graduation Grandma

I'd rather learn from one bird how to sing
than teach ten thousand stars how not to
dance.

—*E. E. Cummings*

Deborah visited me the following year in the spring,
when the desert was blooming. We took pictures of
each other and enjoyed shopping and sharing the
events of the previous year. Did we look alike? Not
really. Sometime later, relatives and friends said our
smiles, our stance, and the way we used our hands
were like Siamese twins.

During the last evening of her visit, she leaned
across the dinner table, a penetrating look on her face. I
was thinking about us, she said. It's interesting that the
baby you gave life to in San Francisco all those years
ago came back and rescued you from a big mistake,
helped to make a different life for you.

I reached for her hand and gave it a squeeze. It was one of the few times we had touched.

❧

I spent that summer of 2005 as I always did then, back in Madison. I returned to Tucson in the fall. Finally, my days were beginning to feel normal again. I could listen to music that used to make me cry. Now I hummed along with the melodies the way I used to. I'd even gained a little weight. I wasn't hiding anymore.

One early evening that fall, as the sun dropped below the serrated purple horizon of the Tucson mountains, I was sitting near my kitchen window pondering my to-do list, when the phone rang. It was Lexa.

Mom, I have some super news. You might want to sit down.

I *am* sitting down. My heart was pounding.

I'm pregnant! You're going to be a grandmother. Her voice was full and bright. We talked about pregnancies and babies. Lexa chattered excitedly, explaining to me how to follow her monthly progress on her website. What a difference from when I birthed Ethan and Lexa, to say nothing of Deb.

The next day I bought two knitted baby bonnets—one trimmed in blue, the other in pink—so as to be ready for whoever it would be. We began weekly phone calls so I could stay informed on how everything was going and share the excitement with her. Every few weeks, I checked her website. By Valentine's Day, she'd posted her twenty-week expectant contour. I started to tremble as I felt some fleeting stillness settle deep within me with such force that I had to catch my breath. I felt I had seen the ground of all being in the miracle of her pregnant profile.

ભ

On my return to Madison in May 2006, I stopped to spend a few days with Lexa and Stephen. Lexa greeted me with her pregnant belly and a big smile, but there were traces of tiredness around her eyes and mouth. I settled on the living-room couch to visit.

Come here, I said, patting my legs and looking up at Lexa. Sit on my lap. I want to hold you.

Mom! I'm way too heavy for that now, she protested.

Oh no, you're not. You're never too heavy or too old to be held.

She gave me her quizzical *oh Mother* look. Okay, but I'll squish you.

I'm pretty tough, even if I'm not very big. I felt her pregnant body next to me as I put my arms around her.

Hey, Stephen, come look at this. Mom's holding me.

He clicked the camera as I felt Lexa's round tummy and slowly moved my fingertips over her t-shirt. Hmm, right here it's very hard.

Yeah, I think that's the butt, but it could be the head.

There's a miracle in there, I said, patting her swollen belly again. Making a miracle is a fine thing to do.

Her face relaxed, the tightness gone for the moment. She was beautiful with her dark-auburn hair framing her milk-white complexion and her hazel eyes.

Like Lexa, I also had a due date. Mine was my fifty-year high-school reunion at the boarding school I had attended when I was not yet thirteen. Driving east from Wisconsin through the Allegany Mountains, I watched the fog feeling its way through the trees. As I approached the river, the mist lifted, and bright green leaves stood out against the cinnamon-colored tree bark. The mountains became hills, and the forests transformed into green meadows. Storm clouds, which were with me most of the car trip, lifted, and the widest rainbow I had ever seen spread across the valley.

I felt like I was seventeen again, ready to graduate and prepared to take on the world. But many years had passed, and I had been through my own emotionally challenging and protracted version of hell—not the journey I had anticipated. Sometimes I felt like giving up and retreating into a solo life, like joining a nunnery. But I couldn't picture myself as a nun. My children inspired me to keep going. I didn't want to let them down. I didn't want them to think I was a wimp. So, I muddled through and learned a lot more about myself.

With renewed energy and the understanding and love of friends, I found my way back to the effective, quick-thinking, passionate young woman who had left this school years ago, eager to seize every moment life had to offer. I arrived in time to join my classmates as we walked together along the stony path to a garden near the old brick mansion, which was the senior dorm. There we planted a white dogwood tree in memory of our classmates who had passed on.

As tender words of remembrance were spoken, I searched the group for familiar faces. Most of the women I hadn't seen for many years, since graduation. Now and then, I recognized a profile, the same dark curly hair now streaked with gray, a remembered posture, a telltale gesture of the hand. As if by magic, a half-century was swept away, and their faces were smooth and young again.

We broke into small groups as we wandered back to the middle school for a glass of wine before dinner. Eagerly, we all began to update each other on our lives. I shared my personal news first with Eleanor, my freshman-year roommate. I heard something about you having a difficult divorce, she announced as she approached me.

You could say that. After thirty-five years of marriage, I discovered that my ex, who had told me he was a sex addict, forgot to tell me he was gay. Just before our divorce was final, I learned he was messing around with boys and men of all ages.

She looked at me with wide eyes and paused to take a sip of wine.

He was a physician and an Episcopal priest, I added.

That's not okay. She shook her head.

You're right. It isn't. I was relieved that she was interested in learning what had happened.

Seems he was a mighty dissembler, she said, running her fingers around the rim of her glass.

Indeed. But not the only one.

Of course not. Look at the Roman Church....

We began to talk about all the many lies and cover-ups that had occurred, and that kept occurring, not only in the church, but also in government, the private sector, wherever there was a patriarchy, it seemed. I told Eleanor how it took my attorney twenty-two months to get me the equivalent of an annulment from my local Episcopal bishop.

That seems a bit tardy on his part. Eleanor shook her head. Whatever happened to your ex?

He's suspended and remains so, I think.

She asked me why he wasn't deposed. I told her that question was never answered for me either. That's stonewalling, she said, frowning. Don't let them get away with that.

I'm trying not to, I promised as we headed for the dining hall.

The room reverberated with the sound of women's voices in earnest discussion and laughter as we moved among the tables, comparing notes and catching up. It was as though we'd been away for an extended weekend and now, gathering like bees at the hive, we were eager to share with one another.

I fell asleep that night exhausted but happy, after reading the memory book that had been assembled by our class. Out of a group of eighty-seven, most had answered a questionnaire, sent in vignettes about their lives, and shared what they remembered most from the years we'd spent together at school. As I read their stories, I was moved by how compassionate and gifted a group of women they were. Most had married and had families. Some had become clerics, lawyers, or doctors. Many had volunteered in nonprofit organizations of all kinds. Some had lost children, others had struggled gallantly against illnesses, and a few had lost loved ones to AIDS. When I finally closed the memory book, it was well past midnight. I hadn't shared my entire story with all of them, not yet. I prayed for poise and courage. It was harder to tell the truth to those close to me than to strangers.

The next day, we visited classes in session. Like many schools in the United States, ours had become coed in the Seventies, and that was the single most obvious change for our class. As I watched the young girls and boys engaged in seminars and sports, I thought about how many of my class had chafed under the rigid expectations held by our parents' generation and those of our grandparents' as well. It was more than sheer adolescent rebellion that urged us to explore and to demand more opportunities than we'd been offered. We sensed, I think, a movement that was about to happen, but we couldn't have identified it then.

As we finished lunch, the reunion coordinator asked us to assemble for a class picture. Thirty of us gathered on the platform. Betty, who drove down from Maine and pitched a tent behind the main school building, brought her dog, a German shepherd, who parked himself in the front row.

It seemed like graduation day again, only this time without long white dresses and bouquets—a dozen red roses tied with pale-blue satin ribbons. No strains of Elgar's "Pomp and Circumstance" music followed us as we walked through the school's arched doorway and onto the grass to take our places in front of the great hall. That was fifty years ago. Now we wore slacks, fashion jeans, and brightly colored jackets. Some wore glasses. Many kept their high-school hairstyles, now streaked with gray or touched with highlights of gold and bronze.

After the photo session, our class met in the wood-paneled alumnae room of the main building. It had been off limits to us when we were students, so it had a certain mysterious and forbidden feel about it. We closed the french doors and arranged ourselves in a big circle. Three large oil portraits hung in the room: two of the women who had started the school—sisters—and their brother. What grimaces they had on their faces. One classmate pointed out that our faculty had an arrogant distance about them, not unlike those of the portraits that hung in the alumnae room, with all their stern expressions that were uncompromising, dismissive, and afraid of our vitality and budding female sexuality.

Alice, who was sitting cross-legged on the window bench, began to speak in a voice hardly more than a whisper. Most of my memories are a negative blur, she said. You all probably remember that I had a friend in upper class, but my roommates warned me that they'd never speak to me again if I kept that friendship. The headmistress called me into her office, and then she called my family. They insisted that I not see her anymore. Her narrow shoulders sagged as she let out a long sigh. The word "homosexuality" wasn't even in our vocabulary, she continued. Certainly not the words "gay" or "lesbian," but that's what they thought, and they were mean and awful. I had to account for every minute I spent out of class. Our friendship wasn't about that. I don't think I'll ever forget how I was treated.

Several classmates shook their heads. Jennifer, seated across the room from me, wiped her eyes. How ignorant and cruel we could be, I thought.

We were just kids, someone added.

That's for sure, said Lucia. There was so much negativity from those old maids. I think some of what happened to us was emotional abuse.

In the late Fifties, this school was like a convent, commented Meredith, her hair pearl white now. We were in an emotional cocoon, not fully aware of what was going outside these "hallowed walls."

Well, I was raising three kids, said Helen. I don't know about you all, but I slept through the Sixties issues, woke up in the Seventies. And then I got involved in environmental concerns.

I think we were right on the edge of the women's movement, Eleanor began as she pulled her chair forward. We were the first class to be exposed to it, really. When we hit college, women's lib was hardly mentioned, but when we left, it was everywhere. The administration and faculty here lost out. I don't think they even knew it was going to happen, but I think most of them at some level were jealous of us. Maybe not consciously, but they sensed that we'd have choices they'd never have.

Liz sat up straight in her seat next to the window and said, Regardless of what they knew or didn't know, we weren't prepared for what was coming. I think a lot of us left with very little self-esteem. I know I did.

I did too, Evelyn, my senior-year roommate, chimed in. It wasn't until much later that I learned that women could be strong, articulate, and even bright.

Amen, said a chorus of voices.

I listened to these memories of melancholy, distress, and accumulated life experiences that my classmates had carried for years. Openly and honestly, they shared their stories, speaking of chronic illnesses and tangled dreams. My heart was racing. I was petrified of their judgment, yet if I couldn't tell *these* women—my classmates, my sisters—the truth of what I'd experienced, I had no business writing a memoir that others would read.

I have some things I want to share with all of you, I heard myself say as I began my story of Deborah, my oldest daughter, whom I had given up for adoption. I leaned forward from my chair, and steadying myself with my elbows, I rested my chin on my hands. My voice quivered as I began. Several of you already know, my marriage of thirty-five years ended when I discovered my husband was a sex addict and gay. I explained how I constructed a new family from the ashes of emotional destruction. As I finished sharing my story, I felt relieved and whole.

Throughout the remainder of the day and evening, several classmates revealed their own accounts of loss and grief and thanked me for my courage and willingness to share. One classmate grabbed my arm and said, You did well! Others gave me prolonged hugs and looked at me with eyes that told me they had also been hurt and healed. Eleanor tapped me on the shoulder.

I have a poem to send you, she said and then waved good-bye, sending me the peace sign as she left.

A package was waiting for me on the doorstep when I returned from my reunion weekend. Deborah had emailed me prior to Mother's Day, alerting me that she was working on a special gift that she wanted me to have before Lexa's baby was born. I wondered why would it be important for me to have it at that time, but I'd learned a lot about Deb over our years of correspondence, and knew she only did things with a clear sense of purpose.

Eagerly, I opened the present and saw a framed photo of Deb's family, all with their smiles ready to burst into laughter. Something else was in the box. I pulled it out and opened the first page of a photo album. On the first page was a picture of Deborah and me, taken when we first had dinner together in 2004. Attached beside it was a small black and white photo of her in 1960—barely a toddler, with lots of curly hair, sitting on a step. She looked just like photos of Lexa and me at the same age. Turning the pages, Deb's life unfolded before me—each photo one year older than the next. There was one of her in a long party dress, looking about twelve. Her hair hung in ringlets to her shoulders. Another pictured her riding a horse.

After photos of Deborah, there were ones of her daughter, Victoria. Her birthdate and weight were written on a pink card, followed by her first baby picture and snaps of her from ages one to nineteen. I stared at the baby photo of my oldest grandchild. Until that moment, I hadn't entirely absorbed the fact that I was already a grandmother. A lot of time had passed, but here in front of me was something I could hold, a photo record that helped fill in what I had missed. There was a section for Deborah's elder son, Dylan, with his birthdate and weight written on a blue card. There were snapshots of him year after year, until sixteen. And then there was her youngest, Todd, another blue card and photos of him grinning ear to ear from ages one to twelve. I closed the album and held it to my breast. These were all the bonus grandbabies, as Deb had called them when I first met them the year before. They come, she'd said when we first met, without any work. They've known about you since they were old enough to know, so in a way they've always known you.

I called Deborah that evening. Your incredible gift arrived. I can't believe I'm holding all these babies in my life. It's hard to grasp all at once, I said, still in awe of what the gift represented.

I know that. Three bonuses all at once are a lot, she said. And you have another one coming soon. That's why I wanted you to have their history to enjoy before the next one arrives. I thought it would be important, being a grandmother and all.

I ached, wishing I could phone my parents to share with them my incredible news: I had three bonus grandchildren, and my first grandchild, Lexa's baby, was only weeks from being born. I picked up Saucer, who was purring under my chair. She was warm and let me snuggle her against me as I cried. This time it was for joy.

Deborah had brought me into her life and drawn a circle completely around us, not excluding her parents, but making a circle that was complementary to them. Then she shared the lives of my bonus grandchildren with me, preparing me to become a grandmother for Lexa's baby. The pieces of a new puzzle were now falling together—just enough for me to see where they fit in my family picture. Soon I'd be holding a newborn grandchild in my arms. Deb had shared her greatest gifts with me. Now I waited for Lexa's.

Two weeks later, early in the morning, Lexa called to say that her baby was breech and that the doctor would try to externally manipulate the baby into the headfirst position prior to her going into labor. I winced at the thought. It wasn't long before my phone rang again.

Mom, I'm in the hospital. Lexa's voice was thin and distant. I'm scheduled for a C-section in about four hours. My placenta isn't working right, and the doctors want to get the baby now.

Okay, I understand. Everything will be fine. Remember, I love you, I said, stuffing my fist in my mouth to keep from crying. I was terrified that something would go wrong.

An hour crept by as I paced the kitchen floor, all the while thinking of Lexa and her baby. It was early afternoon when a nurse called to tell me Lexa was out of the operating room. A baby girl had been born. That was all she would tell me. A short time later, the phone rang. I heard Lexa's voice announce joyfully, I'm okay, Mom, and so is Rebekkah.

That's wonderful. When can I see you all?

Oh, give us ten days or so. We need to get acquainted.

I packed my suitcase and was on my way as soon as Lexa said Rebekkah was ready for visitors. The sweet scent of a honey-locust tree greeted me as I walked up their front walk. Lexa stood in the doorway, holding Rebekkah over her shoulder, patting her gently. I followed her into the living room and sat on the edge of their sofa. I held out my arms, and she handed Rebekkah to me. For a moment I was tentative, and then I snuggled her close to me as I studied her pink-perfect skin, her tiny turned-up nose, her infant hands with nails so small I could barely see them. She was dreaming, and then as if on cue, the right side of her perfect mouth curved upward and she smiled. Suddenly I was laughing, crying, and praying all at once. My family, which I thought I had lost, was whole. I had a son and a daughter-in-law who cared for me enough to let me fall apart on their watch and then helped me find my way again. I had a daughter and a son-in-law who made me a granny for the first, and the fourth, time. And I had a special friend who believed in bonus grandchildren.

I remembered that at my high-school reunion the previous month, one of my high-school classmates— whose husband had died twenty years earlier—had stopped me as we were saying good-bye. Isn't it interesting what we find when we lose something? She was right: it was amazing grace I found when I thought I had lost my way.

Epilogue

The future is the call to the desert of life through which we all must pass before the desert can bloom within us.

—Chittister and Williams

In the summer of 1963, I had decided that working in a physician's office wasn't going to satisfy me. I had seen nurses working in the postop recovery room after patients had open-heart surgery, and I wanted to be one of those nurses. I had graduated from UC Berkeley in 1961. Surely the UC San Francisco Medical Center would accept me. It offered a bachelor's degree in nursing, and I was already living in the city.

After my appointment with an admissions officer, I learned the curriculum my class would be pursuing would be the subject of a research project. An investigator was trying to establish that certain kinds of learning methods had a high probability of producing change agents.

We were a class of about forty students, all of whom had fulfilled their prenursing courses: anatomy, physiology, chemistry, bacteriology, and biology. On the first day of classes, as we sat together in the small auditorium dressed in our blue-and-white pinstriped student-nurse uniforms, I sensed my degree was not going to make any difference, given what we were about to encounter. It was hoped that the new program being tested would inspire us to become change agents, regardless of where we applied our nursing skills.

Years later, after returning to California in 2009, I attended a nursing-school weekend reunion with one of my colleagues. About twenty-five of us arrived in time for dinner. After forty years, I wasn't certain that I could put together all the names and faces. It was early February, and we gathered in front of a large fireplace in the living room of an old house turned retreat center, ready to share our experiences since last we met. Because I'd never been to our reunion before, I was allotted ten minutes to bring my classmates up to date rather than the usual five.

Reunion retreats usually begin with catching up, so I had a handout to pass around: my bio, my elevator pitch, and the chapter headings of my memoir. I figured that about covered it. What I really wanted to share with my classmates was how my birth daughter had found me and become part of my life. Now that I was almost finished writing my memoir, I didn't want to keep any more secrets.

As I was packing up my overnight bag, getting ready to leave that Sunday morning, Sally, one of my classmates, poked her head into my room. Hesitantly, she walked toward me, her arms outstretched as she said in a shaky voice, I'm a birth mother too. I hugged her. Have you found your child? I said. Sally shook her head no, adding that she carried a big hole in her heart. Quickly brushing away her tears, she explained she'd had a baby boy and commented that probably men didn't really want to be found. I asked her if she'd like to try to find him anyway, and when she answered yes, I gave her Deb's e-mail address. Within thirty-eight hours, I received a phone call from Sally. Her son was registered at the website Deb suggested, and Sally had already talked with him. She said I had changed her life and she didn't know how to thank me. I told her the best way was to pay it forward. And then I choked up as I realized what had happened: my story was the instrument of positive change in someone's life. I had become a change agent, just as the nursing school had hoped. My wish is that my experience will be the same for others.

☙

Five years earlier, I'd met a man, a tall, lanky kind of guy. He wore a cowboy hat and boots and drove a silver sports car. Sometimes he wore a baseball hat. When he wasn't being a geologist, Nathan was a sailor and a serious tinkerer. His garage was filled with tools and a metallic blue '52 Ford pickup that he was rebuilding.

We took a honeymoon to Europe, crossing the Atlantic on a ship of course—I still don't like to fly—and got married when we returned home. The ceremony took place in the same church where I had spent that sad and lonely day back in 1959.

But this time, with joy in my heart, I stood within the shadows at the back of the church and watched as Nate and his daughter took their places at the right side of the altar next to his two best friends. Suddenly the aisle looked very long. My daughter–in–law, Angela, dressed in burgundy red and six months pregnant, walked down the aisle first. Following her was my daughter, Lexa, dressed in purple, holding eighteen-month-old Rebekkah in her arms. A few seconds later, I began to walk toward Nathan. I heard the organ playing the music we had chosen and saw a multitude of people looking at me. I was shaking, and although I tried to smile, my eyes still filled with tears, and my lips trembled. As I reached the altar, Nathan walked toward me. The priest whispered to him, Breathe, Nate, breathe.

We celebrated our ninth wedding anniversary this year. Nathan continues to be a consulting geologist. We have six grandchildren to enjoy. I hope to write some stories for our younger ones, and I look forward to returning to my weaving and the rhythm of my loom.

Afterword

On a cool morning in mid-February, as the sun played hide-and-seek with the gray clouds hovering over the Catalina Mountains, my postal carrier delivered mail to the front door. Catch you tomorrow, she said, quickly handing me a slim packet of letters. A plain, business-sized envelope caught my eye. It was dated February 14, 2004. It was from Mark.

I thought we'd finished everything long ago. As I slit open the envelope, I heard my heart beating in my ears. I couldn't catch my breath. In the letter Mark admitted doing some things he knew had hurt me, and then he asked if I could forgive him for some of the pain he had caused me. Just *some*? Hadn't our entire marriage been a lie?

What exactly did he mean—that he was sorry for certain acts or events throughout our lives together but not the underlying fact that he lied to our children and me about who he really was? He must have known that his emotional absence made it impossible for us to connect with him. I didn't think forgiveness worked that way, picking and choosing which words and deeds to forgive. I thought it meant *all* those things, like in the Lord's Prayer, "forgive us our sins, as we forgive those who sin against us."

Thoughts about forgiveness had been bothering me since shortly after our divorce, in December 2000. The priest at the church I was attending in Southern California in 2001, Father Shaw, had quickly determined that I was in a mighty battle. We met several times during those late-winter months as he encouraged me to learn about forgiveness. I knew that if I was ever to be at peace with myself, I would have to let go of Mark, and that meant forgiving him. At the time, the best I could do was to ask God to forgive Mark. Maybe that was enough; let God do the forgiving, because I couldn't.

One time, after a discussion with Father S., I remembered something Nelson Mandela had said about there being no healing for victims until they had been heard. Years passed, and after many struggles with writing my own story, the pieces finally fit together. Working my way to forgiveness was the reason I had to write the memoir, not only to forgive Mark, but also to forgive myself for all the mistakes I made along the way. In the end, it wasn't about Mark; it was about me. I had to learn how to forgive myself.

ༀ

It was a warm day in mid-July 2014, and I was at home in Wisconsin. Nate was out of town and nearby friends had invited me to meet them at the Episcopal church by the lake where Mark and I had worshipped together years ago. The organ had stopped playing, the congregation silent during the quiet time at the end of the communion service. Suddenly I heard a small voice say, I forgive you. I didn't think I'd said it, but there it was. Had I forgiven Mark? Or me? Or perhaps both of us? I understood then that the words were mine, whispered under my breath. I had worked many years to smooth the rough edges of forgiveness; it was a process I was learning.

It takes a long time.

ೞ

Revised versions of the Constitution and Canons of the Episcopal Church were adopted during their 2015 general convention in Salt Lake City. These guiding documents contain directives that improve the organization's response to misconduct, such as that described in this memoir. My hope is that the church's response to future wrongdoings will be initiated swiftly, with compassion and respect.

Suggested Reading

When I first learned of Mark's "problem" I went straight to the nearest bookstore. It was 2000 and I couldn't find anything to read on the subject. What was available, I later learned, was not filed under the headings: straight or gay. Since that time many relevant books have been written. These are some that were helpful to me, along with other selected publications related to the issues at hand.

Arnett, Jeffery Jensen, PhD and Elizabeth Fishel
    Getting to 30: A Parent's Guide to the
        20-Something Years. New York: Workman
        Publishing, 2014.

Boss, Pauline
    Ambiguous Loss: Learning to Live with
        Unresolved Grief. Cambridge, Massachusetts:
        Harvard University Press, 2000.

Buxton, Amity Pierce PhD
    The Other Side of the Closet: The Coming-Out
       Crisis for Straight Spouses and Families.
       Hoboken, New Jersey: Wiley Publishing, 1994.

Carnes, Patrick, PhD
    Out of the Shadows: Understanding Sexual
       Addiction. Center City, Minnesota: Hazelden
       Information & Education Services, 2001.

Carnes, Sefanie Editor, PhD
    Mending a Shattered Heart: A Guide for Partners
       of Sex Addicts. Arizona: Gentle Path Press,
       2011.

Corley, M. Deborah, PhD and Jennifer P. Schneider,
    MD, PhD
    Disclosing Secrets: When, to Whom, and How
       Much to Reveal. North Charleston, South
       Carolina: CreateSpace, 2012.

Grever, Carol, MA
    My Husband is Gay: A Woman's Guide to
       Surviving the Crisis. Berkeley, California:
       Crossing Press, 2011.

James, John W. and Russell Freidman
    The Grief Recovery Handbook. New York:
       William Morrow Paperbacks, 2017.

Kaye, Bonnie
> *Straight Wives: Shattered Lives*, Philadelphia,
> Pennsylvania: Bonnie Kaye Services, 2007.

Kennedy, Sheila Rauch
> *Shattered Faith*. New York: Pantheon Books,
> 1997.

Meredith, Lydia
> *The Gay Preacher's Life: How My Gay Husband
> Deconstructed My Life and Reconstructed My
> Faith*. New York: Gallery Books, 2016.

Schneider, Jennifer P., MD, PhD
> *Back from Betrayal: Recovering from the Trauma
> of Infidelity*. North Charleston, South
> Carolina: CreateSpace, 2015.

Schneider, Jennifer P., MD, PhD and M. Deborah
Corley, PhD
> *Surviving Disclosure: A Partner's Guide for
> Healing the Betrayal of Intimate Trust*. North
> Charleston, South Carolina: CreateSpace,
> 2012.

Resources

Resources and statistics of interest to this book are listed here in alphabetical order by content. The information provided herein consists of selected excerpts quoted directly from the referenced websites. You may read more about these subjects by searching the sites provided. The dates provided here are the times when I located the information. Some of this statistical information will certainly change in the future.

ANXIETY AND PANIC DISORDERS

National Alliance on Mental Illness (NAMI)
https://www.nami.org/Learn-More/Mental-Health-Conditions/Anxiety-Disorders
An overview of anxiety disorders as mental health issues, followed by a discussion of treatment options and access to support and other resources.

CHILD ABUSE

American Society for the Positive Care of Children
www.americanspcc.org/child-abuse-statistics
Data provided regarding the abuse and neglect of children in the United States.

Survivors Network of those Abused by Priests (SNAP)
http://www.snapnetwork.org
"SNAP is an independent, confidential network of survivors of institutional sexual abuse and their supporters who work to: protect the vulnerable, heal the wounded, and expose the truth."

U.S. Department of Health & Human Services
Child Welfare Information Gateway
https://www.childwelfare.gov/topics/systemwide/statistics
Overview of abuse problem and access to mitigation resources.

HIV/AIDS

Centers for Disease Control & Prevention (CDC)
https://www.cdc.gov/hiv/basics/statistics.html
Statistics and supporting information regarding extent of HIV/AIDS epidemic in United States.

United Nations AIDS Program
www.unaids.org/en/resources/fact-sheet
Overview of HIV/AIDS statistics and trends worldwide.

HOMOSEXUALITY IN THE UNITED STATES

Pew Research Center
www.pewforum.org/religious-landscape-study/views-about-homosexuality
Summary of nationwide views and trends regarding homosexuality, based on religious affiliation.

Wikipedia - Demographics of Sexual Orientation
https://en.wikipedia.org/wiki/Demographics_of_sexual_orientation
A comprehensive, worldwide treatise, with data regarding demographics in the United States.

INTERPERSONAL RELATIONSHIP TRAUMA

Center for Motivation & Change
https://motivationandchange.com/why-are-relationships-so-hard-understanding-and-overcoming-interpersonal-trauma
The facts about trauma and access to treatment.

Partners of Sexual Addicts Resource Center (PoSARC)
http://www.posarc.com/infidelity/interpersonal-relational-trauma-irt
Definition of interpersonal relational trauma as form of PTSD, with links to resources and support.

THE NEW MIXED MARRIAGE

Wikepedia – Mixed Orientation Marriage
https://en.wikipedia.org/wiki/Mixed-orientation_marriage
Contains a discussion of marriages that contain one straight spouse and one gay partner, and the underlying dynamics involved.

SEXUAL ADDICTION

American Society of Addiction Medicine (ASAM)
https://www.asam.org
"ASAM, founded in 1954, is a professional medical society representing over 5000 physicians, clinicians and associated professionals in the field of addiction medicine. ASAM is dedicated to increasing access and improving the quality of addiction treatment, educating physicians and the public, supporting research and prevention, and promoting the appropriate role of physicians in the care of patients with addiction."

COSA
http://www.cosa-recovery.org
"COSA is a Twelve Step recovery program for men and women whose lives have been affected by compulsive sexual behavior."

Sex Addicts Anonymous (SAA)
https://saa-recovery.org
"As a fellowship of recovering addicts, Sex Addicts Anonymous offers a message of hope to anyone who suffers from sex addiction."

Society for the Advancement of Sexual Health (SASH)
http://www.sash.net
SASH is "a nonprofit multidisciplinary organization dedicated to scholarship, training, and resources for promoting sexual health and overcoming problematic sexual behaviors."

SLEEP APNEA

Mayo Clinic
https://www.mayoclinic.org/diseases-conditions/sleep-apnea/basics/definition/con-20020286
An in-depth evaluation of the health risks associated with sleep apnea.

National Institute of Health (NIH)
https://www.nhlbi.nih.gov/health/health-topics/topics/sleepapnea
An overview regarding the diagnosis, health effects and treatment options for sleep apnea.

UNITED STATES SUICIDE STATISTICS

American Foundation for Suicide Prevention (AFSP)
https://afsp.org/about-suicide/suicide-statistics
Data regarding the U.S. suicide rate, and occurrence for several socio-economic, ethnic and racial groups.

Wikipedia – Suicide in the United States
https://en.wikipedia.org/wiki/Suicide_in_the_United_States
A summary that discusses the suicide rate, and the number by age group and gender.

Margherita Gale Harris, RN, MSN, MPH

In her work as a memoirist, Margherita Gale Harris draws on her career as a registered nurse, specializing in psychiatric nursing and public health. Following a BA in psychology from the University of California at Berkeley, she received a BS in nursing with a public health emphasis from the University at San Francisco Medical Center. Gale alternated her continuing education with positions at private and public hospitals, as well as nonprofit organizations, including Planned Parenthood, Suicide Prevention, Parents under Stress, and Women in Recovery. While practicing her profession, she obtained a MS in psychiatric nursing, with a minor in teaching at Case Western Reserve University, a MPH in Public Health from the University of California at Berkeley, and training at the Gestalt Institute of Cleveland. Gale is the mother of three and grandmother of six. As an accomplished photographer and fabric weaver, she continues to pursue her love of natural color and design. She happily remarried in 2007.

Made in the USA
Lexington, KY
23 August 2018